# THE HAUNTING OF
# ALABAMA

# THE HAUNTING OF
# ALABAMA

## ALAN BROWN

**PELICAN PUBLISHING COMPANY**
GRETNA 2017

*The word "Pelican" and the depiction of a pelican are trademarks of Pelican Publishing Company, Inc., and are registered in the U.S. Patent and Trademark Office.*

ISBN: 9781455622900
E-book ISBN 9781455622917

Printed in the United States of America

Published by Pelican Publishing Company, Inc.
1000 Burmaster Street, Gretna, Louisiana 70053

*To my ghost magnet,*
*Marilyn*

# Contents

# Preface

My love affair with the supernatural side of Alabama began in 1990 when I started transcribing interviews collected for the Works Progress Administration in the late 1930s by a resident of Livingston named Ruby Pickens Tartt. She traveled through the red-clay hills of West Alabama in search of subjects, most of whom were African-American sharecroppers and domestic servants. I was struck by the fact that many of these true accounts contained stories of encounters with ghosts. The sincerity with which the narrators told these tales makes them even more disturbing.

Around the same time that I was working on the Tartt manuscripts, I began reading the works of another Alabama folklorist, Kathryn Tucker Windham. Her collections of Alabama ghost stories—such as *13 Alabama Ghosts and Jeffrey* (1969) and *Jeffrey's Latest 13: More Alabama Ghosts* (1982)—contain tales that earned her acclaim as Alabama's foremost authority on the state's ghost lore. Many of her tales are now regarded as the definitive versions of the stories. I had the great privilege of knowing Kathryn. In 1994, she agreed to serve as a guest speaker in a summer seminar I was teaching on folklore. Our friendship deepened over the next seventeen years. She was featured several times as a guest speaker at the Sucarnochee Folklife Festival. I had the privilege of driving her there from her home in Selma. I will never forget the stories she told me about places I had passed by a hundred times on Highway 80 and never given a second thought to. On my trips with her, I received a crash course in Alabama folklore and folk life.

*The Haunting of Alabama* features stories collected from the entire state. Alabama is rich in folktales, so I decided to include the ones that are closely tied to the state's history. This book includes updates of some of Kathryn's stories. I also chose tales that are compelling but not known outside of a particular community or region. My goal was to include as many personal interviews as I could. Thanks to a professional-development grant I received from the University of Alabama, I was able to travel throughout the state and interview waitresses, desk clerks, professors, and anyone else who had had a paranormal experience or knew someone who had.

As the number of ghost stories grew, I was forced to reassess my view of a haunted place. Houses are not the only places where spirits dwell. They can be found any place where human beings have lived and worked, including hospitals, hotels, restaurants, universities, battleships, farms, and valleys. Alabama's ghost lore reflects the experience of the people who lived and told the tales. The stories are depositories of the history and values of Alabamians. While Alabama's ghost stories share motifs common to many tales in the South, they also contain elements that any resident of the state can recognize as being "pure Alabama."

The reader will notice that many of the stories in this book include investigations by paranormal investigators. Even though I have participated in ghost hunts throughout the South, my intention is not to prove that ghosts are real. People who are buying electromagnetic-field (EMF) meters, voice recorders, and thermal imagers are contributing to the storylines that people will continue telling for generations. The best ghost stories describe incidents that cannot be proved or disproved by anyone, including ghost hunters, scientists, psychologists, or historians. They raise the question, "Could this really have happened?" and haunt the reader's dreams.

# Acknowledgments

I'd like to thank Connie Lawson, librarian at the Demopolis Public Library, who assisted me with my research on Gaineswood and Bluff Hall. I am also indebted to Michelle Bunnich, who told me about the ghost stories connected with the Freight House Restaurant. I am thankful to my colleagues Kendrick Prewitt and Lesa Shaul for taking a detour to the campus of the University of North Alabama during the Literary Odyssey Trip. Not only did Joyce Perrin give me tours of the Josephine Hotel and the Pauly Jail in Union Springs, but she also sent me a great deal of information on the former. Greg Jones, my friend and colleague, proved once again to be of great assistance with his technical expertise. Finally, I would like to thank my wife, Marilyn, who provided invaluable assistance during my story-collecting forays into Alabama.

# THE HAUNTING OF
# ALABAMA

# Chapter 1

# Haunted Houses

### Baldwin Hill
### Livingston

Julian Ennis built the house on Baldwin Hill in 1901. Sometime in the first half of the twentieth century, people began telling ghost stories about the home. A poem written by Mrs. W. H. Coleman addresses the house's haunted reputation. Using a maid as a narrator, Coleman highlighted some of the reported activity at the home. She mentioned that the porch swing moved back and forth. The ghost on Baldwin Hill also "shakes de winders" and "knocks right on de do."

Lucy Gallman, the current owner of Baldwin Hill, moved into the house with her family in 1954. She was five years old at the time. She was nurtured on stories about the spooky house that she called home. The first tale she recalled hearing was about the previous tenants. Night after night, they heard a bouncing ball. A few seconds later, a spectral voice would say, "Robert Ennis is dead." Robert Ennis was Julian's nephew. Thinking that somebody was standing on the porch and talking through a window, the family sprinkled cornmeal on the porch, hoping to see footprints in the powder the next morning. That night, they heard the same creepy sounds: the bouncing ball and the ghostly voice saying, "Robert Ennis is dead." However, when they looked out the front window, the cornmeal was completely undisturbed.

The haunted activity is not restricted to the main house. The little cottages down the hill may be haunted as well. In the late 1990s, a college student who was renting one of them threw open the door and ran up to the main house. When Lucy opened her door, she was greeted by the sight of her young tenant shaking uncontrollably. After she settled down, she told Lucy that she was in the kitchen washing dishes when a white figure floated across the floor and passed into another room. The girl was so terrified that she fled the house without even turning off the tap in the kitchen sink.

A female spirit roams the halls of Baldwin Hill, and it is very close to the Gallman family, especially Lucy's husband, Ken. "This is actually the truth," he said. "We were moving. I looked up for a second and my [late] mother-in-law was standing in the door. It was not a glimpse but it was the clear image of her standing there inside the door. She wore a nightgown that was about forty-three thousand years old but it was comfy." Later on, Ken saw the face of Lucy's mother staring at him through a window.

Strong family ties may also be responsible for Lucy's father's

*The ghosts of family members have found it difficult to leave Baldwin Hill permanently.* (Photo by Alan Brown)

return from the "other side." One day, Lucy's granddaughter saw the apparition of an elderly man inside the house. Her description of the old gentleman's appearance matched that of Lucy's father. "She said he had white hair," Lucy noted. "Also, he was wearing a pale-colored suit."

The ghost's attachment to Lucy's family could be behind another paranormal incident that occurred during her niece's wedding. Lucy's father was supposed to attend, but he passed away suddenly shortly before the wedding. Following the ceremony, Lucy and Ken were looking at the photographs taken of the family. On close examination, orbs could be seen hovering over the heads of the newlyweds. To this day, the niece's husband has no intention of ever sleeping inside the mansion.

## The Beavers House
## Cuba

The tranquility of small-town life in Cuba was shattered on May 22, 1978, when two fugitives from an Oklahoma prison—Eugene Dennis and Michael Lancaster, both twenty-five—arrived. They had escaped at 1:45 P.M. on April 23. The pair signed out of their cell block to attend the prison's nondenominational church. Apparently, they sneaked past the chapel and entered a small passageway leading from the old prison mess hall to a new building under construction. They broke their way through the three yards of concrete sealing off an abandoned utility tunnel. Once outside the power plant, they climbed two fifteen-foot chain-link fences and escaped. They stole a red Chevrolet Camaro in Waynesboro. Mississippi, and made their way to Butler, Alabama. On May 16, a Butler policeman named Dean Larsen Roberts spotted a car matching the description of a red Camaro that had been used in the break-in of a local drugstore. He pulled the Camaro over and stopped a few yards behind it. Suddenly, the passenger got out and fired a shotgun five times at Roberts' squad car, blowing out the passenger-side window and hitting the officer in the arm. The escapees ditched the Camaro in a dense patch of woods in Choctaw County and walked over to the home of Emma Mae Williams. No one was there, so Dennis and Lancaster helped themselves to underwear, pillowcases, and canned goods. They also cut the telephone lines and ate dinner. The pair then went to the home of a neighbor, Isabell James, and stole her 1975 Mercury.

On May 22, a sixty-nine-year-old resident of Cuba, Stacey Beavers, arrived at the antebellum home where she lived alone. She parked in front of the house and, carrying a plate of food from the church social she had attended, walked in. Police believe that she was attacked by Dennis and Lancaster as soon as she set foot in the house. The men slashed her throat and left her bloody corpse lying in the doorway. When word of the horrific murder spread, panic swept through Cuba. People made jokes about sleeping with their shotguns.

*On May 22, 1978, sixty-nine-year-old Stacey Beavers was murdered in the hallway of her home.* (Photo by Alan Brown)

Not long after Stacey Beavers' death, officers from Oklahoma drove to Alabama to assist Choctaw County Sheriff Don Lolley with the investigation. The fugitives remained in Alabama for four more days. Finally, on the morning of May 26, the state troopers learned of their location. Dennis and Lancaster stood their ground, killing three troopers before being killed themselves. By the time their reign of terror ended, they had killed eight people, including Stacey Beavers.

Charlie and Linda Munoz purchased the Beavers House and the forty-eight adjoining acres at auction for $72,000 in 1978. They suspect that price was low because of the home's reputation. They had not lived in it for very long before people began driving up their long drive, hoping to catch a glimpse of the murder house. Linda was shocked when she heard that Stacey Beavers' niece was the one who cleaned the blood splatter off the walls of the entranceway.

Charlie and Linda learned about the early history of the house by conducting research and talking to longtime residents of Cuba. "The house was built in 1850 by Steve Potts," Charlie told me. "It was the first plantation in Cuba, which was called Clay Station back then. A dentist named Dr. Beavers bought the house in 1898. He changed the lines of the house to make it more Victorian. He was a traveling dentist. His office was in a little room upstairs. Stacey Beavers was born in the house."

The first indication Charlie and Linda had that their home might be haunted was strange smells. "One night, I woke up, and the smell of strong perfume was right next to my head," Linda said. "It was so strong that it woke me up. I can't tell you what kind of perfume it was. I just know that it was something that I don't wear. I nudged Charlie and said, 'Charlie, do you smell that? Do you smell that?' He woke up, but the smell had drifted away. He would get up in the middle of the night because he thought I had left candles burning. He would walk up and down the halls looking to see where the candles were burning. A year or so after that, one of Stacey Beavers' nieces came to the house and asked, 'Have you ever experienced anything here?' I said, 'Yeah, we would get up in the middle of the night thinking that candles were burning. I have smelled the scent of strong perfume.' The niece got a very strange look and said, 'My aunt loved splashy perfume, and she burned candles all the time.'"

Charlie and Linda soon discovered that Stacey Beavers' spirit may have attached itself to one of the objects in the house. One of the first pieces of furniture they acquired for the home was a piano once owned by Stacey Beavers. "When we first bought the house, Mrs. Brock [a resident of Cuba] was waiting for us in the hall," Linda said. "Mrs. Brock bought the piano with the intention of giving it back to whoever bought the house, and that's how we got Stacey's piano. It came from a bar in Kansas City, the town where she worked as a music therapist." The piano was involved in the most dramatic supernatural incident inside the Beavers House.

"The first really scary event happened about twenty-five years ago [1991]," Linda said. "My son was not born yet, and my daughter was little. I was working at the hospice at the time, and I had been dealing with a really difficult family. The patients were wonderful. It was always the families that gave me the problems. It was a very difficult time. I had been driving night after night from Cuba to Livingston. I was exhausted, and I had promised my daughter that I would have a Halloween party for her. Our friends had children the same age as our child, so we always had family parties: adults and children. Whenever someone came over, they would want to go upstairs. There used to be a belvedere on the top of the house, but now it's just a wall. We had taken a couple up there to see the sky. My husband and I used to watch the stars. A friend of ours from Columbus [Mississippi], Eric Loftis, was playing honkytonk music on the piano while we were walking upstairs. Suddenly, we heard what sounded like a gunshot. We ran back down the stairs, and Eric was standing there with a shocked look on his face. We checked over the house to make sure that none of the children were hurt. Then we noticed that the armoire had fallen over, right next to the piano. We up-righted it and were surprised to discover that none of the glass on the armoire was broken. I took my daughter upstairs to put her to bed. Five minutes later, I went downstairs, and no one was there except Charlie. I asked Charlie, 'Where is everybody?' Charlie said, 'Gone.'" Linda suspects that the armoire fell over because of Stacey Beavers' dislike of honkytonk music.

Stacey Beavers may have expressed her disapproval of changes made in the house during a New Year's Eve party in 2000. "We had a really bad termite infestation," Linda said. "The carpenter working in the kitchen was having to tear out walls and replace sheetrock and the ceiling in the kitchen. He had nailed the boards up and was getting ready to leave just before the party guests arrived. Eric had come from Columbus and had sat down to play piano. When he started, the boards just collapsed onto the kitchen floor! The carpenter said there was no reason for them to fall because they were nailed securely."

During another party, Stacey Beavers may have expressed her displeasure at remarks made by her great-niece. "We sat at the drop-down table," Linda said, "and it had the ends raised up. The subject of Stacey Beavers came up, and her great-niece said, 'Everyone talks about how wonderful Stacey was, but she wasn't perfect.' She went on to talk about disagreements she had had with her great-aunt. Well, after a while, I got up and went to the bathroom, and she went into the kitchen. All of a sudden, the end of the table fell down, and everything that was on it—plates, silverware—fell to the floor. That had never happened before, and it hasn't happened since."

Linda Munoz's nephew, Ed Snodgrass, is an experimental psychologist at the University of West Alabama. He had an experience inside the old house that came into direct conflict with his scientific view of the world. "My family and I were living in Meridian [Mississippi] in a house we restored," Ed told me. "We added a child. The place had one bathroom. We had to sell it in 2008. We sold the house, did well, and about that time, my aunt Linda told me that she and my uncle Charlie were going to move up to the Mentone area, where they had a house. Supposedly, they were going to live there for a while, certainly for a year, and she wondered if we would be interested in housesitting her house on Old Livingston Road—the Beavers House. I've always loved that house."

Ed and his wife, Michelle, moved in and had a great year there. Several months after moving in, they discovered they were going to have their third baby. Cuba is miles from hospitals, and it would have complicated their life somewhat to reside out there. Later, Linda and Charlie decided to return because Linda's mother, living near Cuba, was aging and needed some assistance. So Ed and Michelle chose to move back to Meridian, to a different house.

Toward the end of that summer, they started packing up. "They had bought a house, and they were moving in," Linda said. "Sometimes they stayed at the Beavers House, and sometimes they stayed in town. They kept the dogs in a fenced-in area in Cuba."

"We had pretty much moved out," Ed said. "There were just a few items left in the house that belonged to us. I went back late one night after everyone had gone to sleep. I drove into Cuba around nine or ten at night. I had never had any fears about the place. I was used to it. I had lived there for a year and visited there as a child. Nothing was on my mind. I didn't feel any insecurity going into the house at all. I was going to gather up some Internet equipment. The house was designed to have a major hallway that crisscrosses. You go in and to the right at the end of that hallway is a staircase that leads upstairs to the attic, and beyond the attic is a staircase that leads up to the roof, where the dental office used to be on top. Now, it's a widow's walk. Anyway, I was walking down the hallway, unplugging wires and equipment from underneath a desk, and suddenly, out of nowhere, I felt an incredible chill come over me that I had never had before, and I have never experienced it since. Anytime I talk about it, the chill bumps rise up." He showed me the goosebumps on his arm. "This experience of chills quickly turned into an experience of fear. And just two seconds after feeling that, the dogs outside began to bark incessantly. They had been quiet. So immediately, I jumped up and left. I didn't look back. I felt like maybe something was watching me. I got in the van and went home, and that was that. I told my wife about it, and she thought that was a curious experience for me because I don't tend to have those experiences. I consider myself a scientist. I still don't have any supernatural beliefs."

Since then, Ed has tried to come up with reasonable explanations, to no avail. "The dogs heard it, and we both had that experience, but that seems pretty implausible," he said. "I will say this. The room my two daughters stayed in was in that hallway by the staircase. They told us that it was frightening over there. It is a little bit dark. There was dark woodwork around the stairs. I never felt that way. I always liked that part of the house. I always thought it was one of the most interesting parts of the house."

Despite all of the unsettling occurrences inside the Beavers House, Linda and Charlie have never been afraid to stay in it. "We have a sense that we were supposed to be here," Linda said. "I never felt scared, even when all this stuff happened. Actually, I think it's kind of cool."

## Bluff Hall
## Demopolis

Francis Strother Lyon (1800-82), the first owner of Bluff Hall, was a prominent lawyer and politician in West Alabama. He was a member of one of the most illustrious families in the state at the time. Gen. Edmund Pendleton Gaines and Col. George Strother Gaines were his uncles. In 1817, Francis came to live with Colonel Gaines, who was the Indian agent in St. Stephens. Following his admission to the bar in 1821, Francis married Sarah Serena Glover of Demopolis. In 1832, her parents, Allen and Sarah (Norwood) Glover, built Bluff Hall at 405 North Commissioners Avenue for their daughter and her husband. Francis and Sarah went on to become the parents of six girls and one boy. Because the Lyons owned a number of outlying plantations, they used Bluff Hall as a townhouse. It remained in the Lyon family until October 30, 1907, when A. R. Smith became the new owner. Bluff Hall continued to be used as a single residence until 1948, when it was converted into apartments. The Marengo County Historical Society bought the antebellum home on March 22, 1967, restored it, and opened it to the public as a museum. In

1970, Bluff Hall was added to the National Register of Historic Places. In 1978, it was included in the Alabama Tapestry of Historic Places.

Bluff Hall is one of the region's grandest homes. The brick exterior of the two-story house was covered with stucco. Six two-story brick columns were set on the front portico. Wrought-iron brackets supported a balcony. In the 1840s, the Federal-style home was remodeled in the Greek Revival style through the addition of a large front wing, a louvered gallery on a rear wing, a colonnaded portico, and white paint. The kitchen and dining room were located on the first floor of the rear wing; the second floor contained two bedrooms. The interior of Bluff Hall is equally impressive. The two columns that grace the double parlor were presented to the Lyons as anniversary gifts from Gen. Nathan B. Whitfield and his family, who owned Gaineswood in Demopolis. The house museum also contains Empire and Victorian furniture, antique kitchen utensils, period clothing, a display on local history, a gift shop, and, some say, the ghost of a little boy.

On October 30, 2003, Kathy Leverett, the Demopolis Chamber of Commerce president, her daughter, and some friends spent the night at Bluff Hall. No one had spent the night there since 1967 when it became a museum. As they were getting ready for bed, they heard some noise upstairs. It sounded like a child jumping rope. It went on for a while, and then it would stop. A few minutes after the girls had fallen asleep, it started up again, so Kathy decided she would investigate. As she was walking up the stairs, she felt as if someone was standing next to her. She looked down and was surprised to see a seven- or eight-year-old boy standing on the step. He had long hair and was wearing a nightshirt. Instead of being scared, Kathy was concerned. She sensed that the little boy was looking for his mother. She turned around and walked down the stairs. When she got to the bottom, the mysterious little stranger was gone.

Unsure of what she had really seen, Kathy sat down in a chair on the first floor to collect her thoughts. Suddenly, out of the corner of her eye, she saw the little boy again, this time in front of a big window

*The ghost of an eight-year-old boy has been seen on the stairs inside Bluff Hall.* (Photo from Wikimedia Commons)

looking out toward the road. He had the same wistful expression on his face. After a few seconds, the little boy vanished.

Convinced that she had just made the acquaintance of a visitor from the past, Kathy decided to explore the history of the house to see if a young boy had ever died there. Kirk Brooker, the director of the Marengo County Historical Society, found that on April 29, 1877, the homeowners' grandson, Leonidas Mecklenburg Polk, had died of scarlet fever at the age of eight. Leonidas, who was called "Merk" by his family, was the son of William M. Polk and Ide Lyon Polk and the grandson of Mr. and Mrs. Francis Strother Lyon and Confederate general Leonidas Polk. His mother was expecting a baby in New York, where they lived, so Merk's parents sent him to Demopolis to celebrate Christmas with his grandparents. Merk's mother gave birth in March, and Merk died in April before she had recovered enough to return to Demopolis. He was buried in the

Lyon family plot at Riverside Cemetery. Even in the afterlife, Merk yearns to gaze into his mother's face.

## Burleson-McEntire House
### Decatur

Jesse Whorton used slave labor to build his Greek Revival mansion on a 778-acre land grant near the Tennessee River in 1824. The eighteen-inch walls were covered with Flemish bond, and the Federal-period furnishings turned the house into a showplace. It was used as a temporary courthouse in the 1830s until construction of the first permanent courthouse in Morgan County was completed in 1837.

The ownership of the house changed several times until it was purchased by Aaron Adair Burleson and his wife, Janet Burleson, in the early 1860s. He was the first president of the Tennessee and Alabama Railroad, which eventually became part of the Nashville and Decatur Railroad. During the Civil War, the mansion served as a field hospital and as a command center for both the Confederate and Union armies. In March 1862, Confederate general Albert Sidney Johnston stayed at the home for a short while, reorganizing his army. Burleson contributed to the war effort by becoming a doctor in the Confederate Army.

Following the fall of Vicksburg in June 1863, Union generals Sherman, Grant, and Blair used the mansion as a meeting place. The Union Army is said to have dried their blankets on the iron fence surrounding the property. The fence remains, but Federal soldiers used the original gates as fire grates.

Burleson's family stayed in the house during the Union occupation of Decatur. Relations between the Burlesons and the Union Army were cordial; in fact, Janet Burleson was given passes to travel between the lines until it was discovered that she was smuggling quinine to the Confederate Army in holes bored in her surrey. The house became the headquarters of Union general Granville M. Dodge in

1864 while he was ordering the evacuation of Decatur. His soldiers burned the Burleson family's personal possessions on the front lawn, including Burleson's books. One of his books, a collection of the poetry of Lord Byron, was stolen by a Federal officer and returned to the Burleson family in 1900.

The mansion was one of five Decatur homes that survived the Civil War because it was inside the Union Army's breastworks, built in 1864. After the war, carpetbaggers used the mansion as their base of local operations. In 1869, a Union veteran named Jerome Hinds bought the house. His niece, Grace Hinds, married Lord Curzon, England's viceroy to India. The mansion was converted into a boardinghouse for a while before R. P. McEntire bought it on April 5, 1895. Today, the Burleson-McEntire House is a private residence.

The past has become a permanent fixture inside the home, especially the Civil War. The Battle of Decatur, October 26-29, 1864, took place when Brig. Gen. Robert S. Granger thwarted Lt. Gen. John Bell Hood's attempt to take his army across the Tennessee River and march into central Tennessee to reclaim Nashville. Hood was forced to take his army westward and cross the river at Tuscumbia. By battle's end, the Union Army had lost 155 men, and the Confederate Army had lost 450 men. Legend has it that a Union soldier who was shot by a Confederate sniper was taken to the Union field hospital and then carried to the Burleson house, where he died. At the time, Federal troops were forced to "hunker down" in the face of withering fire from the Confederates, and it was not possible to bury their comrade outside. In desperation, the soldiers ripped up several of the floorboards and deposited the fallen soldier under the house. After the Union Army recaptured the city a few days later, the soldiers removed the corpse from the floor and buried it in the yard.

The first ghost sighting at the Burleson-McEntire House occurred shortly after Jerome Hinds moved in. Hinds' daughter claimed that the most haunted room was her parents' bedroom. One night, her mother awoke to see a dark-haired woman in a white gown standing at the foot of the bed, staring at her intently. She made several more unsolicited visits while the McEntires lived there. Years later, Mrs.

*According to legend, the corpse of a Union soldier was deposited under the floorboards of the Burleson-McEntire House.* (Photo from Pinterest)

Frank Brown's family rented the old house. When she was a girl, she and her sister stayed in the same bedroom where Mrs. Hinds had her sighting, and they saw the lady in white as well. They told their parents that the dark-haired woman was staring at them. They traded bedrooms with their brothers, but the boys did not stay long after the female spirit visited them too. A woman who was staying with the Brown family had her own harrowing experience inside the house. She was about to go to bed when she saw a lighted candle floating above the hallway door. Suddenly, the candle hurtled in her direction and blew up in her face.

Jeremy McEntire had his own paranormal experience at the old house around the turn of the century. He told a newspaper reporter, "I was walking home from grammar school, and when I got to the earth bridge, it's paved now, I looked up at the top of the house and saw Papa. At least, I thought it was him." Jeremy went inside the house and asked his mother why his father was standing on the roof. She replied that Jeremy's father was working several miles away. She and Jeremy were the only two people in the house. Convinced that he really had seen someone on the roof, Jeremy climbed the stairs to the attic and was shocked to find that the doors and windows were locked.

The identity of the male apparition has long been thought to be the unquiet spirit of the Union soldier who died in the house and was buried far from home. However, it could also be the ghost of either of two other men who died violently at the Burleson-McEntire House. One possibility could be a Union paymaster who was delivering wages to the soldiers quartered there. His lifeless body was found lying outside the front gate of the mansion. Apparently, he was murdered and robbed before he could pay the soldiers. The ghost could also be the spirit of a carpetbagger named Judge Carlton, who stayed at the Burleson-McEntire House for a while. Because he was an outspoken critic of the Ku Klux Klan, Carlton received a number of death threats. Fearing for his life, the judge made plans to flee Decatur and seek refuge in Mexico. One day, he went to the bank to withdraw funds for the trip. Shortly after leaving the bank, Carlton was killed somewhere between the railroad depot and the Burleson-McEntire House. Although it was widely assumed that he was murdered by the Ku Klux Klan, his murderers were never brought to justice.

Amateur historian Robert Parkham told me his own theory regarding ghosts at the Burleson-McEntire House. "Now when I was a kid, I used to frequently go to the McEntire house and talk to Mrs. McEntire, and she showed me where the old boards were (of course, new boards had replaced them years before). She said that they put his body under the floor." The young soldier was shot when Confederate snipers were firing down on Union troops from atop the Old State Branch Bank. "After Hood retreated across the Tennessee River, Union troops came back to Decatur and gave the boy's body a proper burial. But his mother grieved herself to death over the loss of her son. Mrs. McEntire said that the ghost in the house is hers, not her son's."

Parkham went on to say that he had a personal encounter with the "ghost" in the home. "As a boy, [my friends and I] used to sit on the curb and wait for the ghost to appear. One night, a light was on in one of the upper rooms facing the street. All of a sudden, the silhouette of this woman walks by. We had seen the ghost! Actually, it was Mrs. McEntire walking through the house."

## Cedarhurst Mansion
## Huntsville

Cedarhurst Mansion is the site of one of Alabama's best-known ghost stories. A wealthy businessman named Stephen Ewing built the house in 1823. He had bought the land on which the mansion stands from Ebenezer Titus. The story goes that in 1837, a fifteen-year-old-girl named Sally Carter visited the home. She was the sister of Ewing's wife, Mary. Sally had been staying in the house for just a few weeks when she became very sick. She succumbed to the disease on November 28, 1837, shortly before her sixteenth birthday. Sally was buried in the backyard, alongside the Ewings' three children.

In 1919, a seventeen-year-old relative of the Ewings from Germantown, Pennsylvania, named Stephen Scott, arrived at Cedarhurst Mansion for a house party over the weekend. On his first night there, he was awakened by the rumbling of a terrible thunderstorm. The young boy was sitting upright in his bed when a young girl in a long, white dress appeared by the window. Frightened out of his wits by what he saw, or thought he saw, he lay back down and closed his eyes. A few minutes later, the boy heard a young girl's voice say, "Help me! Please help me!" When Scott reopened his eyes, he was shocked to see the same tall, dark-haired beauty standing next to his bed. In a spectral voice, she said, "The wind has blown my tombstone over. Please set it up for me." He wondered if it was Sally. The next morning, Scott was eating with his relatives when he informed them of his strange visitation the night before. After the laughter subsided, Scott said, "O.K. Let's go out to her grave and see if Sally's tombstone is still standing upright." Scott and his cousins walked over to Sally's grave and, sure enough, her tombstone was lying on the ground.

In the 1950s and 1960s, spending the night on Sally Carter's grave became a rite of passage for Huntsville teenagers. In December 1982, Sally and the Ewings' three children were exhumed and reburied at Maple Hill Cemetery. The exact location of the graves was never revealed, to protect them from desecration.

At about the same time, a local businessman purchased Stephen Ewing's former home for the purpose of developing the property into a gated community. Today, Cedarhurst Mansion serves as a clubhouse for the residents of the community's private homes and townhouses. It soon became clear that Sally Carter's spirit remained in the house that she had loved to visit back in the early nineteenth century. One night, a security guard heard someone walking around upstairs. Suddenly, she realized that the money she had in her pocket was gone. Thinking that she had lost the money while patrolling the grounds earlier, the woman grabbed her flashlight and left the house through the back door. She had not walked very far when the flashlight began flickering. Frustrated, she returned to the guardhouse, convinced that her money was lost forever. She opened the door, and in the flickering beam of the flashlight, she found her missing money. The security guard breathed a sigh of relief and thanked Sally Carter for helping her out. Almost immediately, she heard the ghostly laughter of a young woman.

A resident of Huntsville named Dorothy Johnson told me of the period when Cedarhurst Mansion was still privately owned. "The owner of the house saw Sally's ghost many times and didn't think anything about it. She was not afraid of her because Sally was not an evil person. One day, a friend of hers came to visit. She [the owner] said, 'Well, take your coat and put it in the upstairs bedroom.' Which she did. And when she came back down, she said, 'Oh, who was that lovely young lady I met on the stairs?' And she [the owner] very nonchalantly said, 'Oh, that was Sally, our ghost,' and went right on."

The Internet has proven to be an invaluable source of information about recent encounters with the spirit of Sally Carter. A number of these stories deal with late-night visits to her grave back when it was still located behind Cedarhurst Mansion. One young woman said that her mother and some friends were in the backyard and saw an apparition of a young girl floating in the air while she was combing her hair. A security guard posted that one night, she heard footsteps inside the house. A few minutes later, a loud noise came from the bathroom, like someone banging on the doors. She walked inside, and the bathroom was completely empty. Who would have thought that a fifteen-year-old girl who died in the 1830s would become an Internet sensation nearly two hundred years later?

## The Cleveland House
## Suggsville

The details of the life of this home's builder, Stephen B. Cleveland, are largely unknown. Birth records indicate that he was born in South Carolina in 1827. His father was a planter named James C. Cleveland. According to a local legend, Stephen went to California during the Gold Rush of 1849 in hopes of striking it rich. Cleveland's story picks up again in 1855, when he married eighteen-year-old Eliza Davis Creagh, the daughter of Gerard Walthal Creagh, a wealthy politician, merchant, and planter. Creagh had served as a representative to the state legislature in 1819, 1820, and 1838 and as a senator in 1839, 1842, and 1847. Shortly after marrying Eliza, Cleveland entered the realm of politics, possibly taking his cue from his father-in-law. Cleveland was elected "Superintendent of Free Public Schools" in 1857 and as state senator in 1859. The next year, Cleveland built his large, one-story house, which combines elements of Greek Revival, Gothic Revival, and Italianate architecture. His home is similar to those built by many members of the planter class just before the Civil War in that it includes both mass-produced and handmade details. The house is distinctive because of its L-shaped plan wrapped in verandas. Samuel Cole, a master builder who lived next door to Cleveland's father, may have been the builder of the Cleveland House, although some of the home's features have led some to believe that Alexander Bragg from Wilcox County was the architect.

The 1860 Federal Census shows that Cleveland was employed as a lawyer and occupied the house with his wife, two children, and eighteen-year-old brother-in-law, Thomas B. Creagh. At the time, his household included forty-two slaves in sixteen slave quarters. Cleveland's brother-in-law owned an additional twenty slaves. Cleveland's extended family lived five houses down the street. These family members included his father, James; his sister, Caroline; his brothers Jeremiah and Alonzo; and his stepbrother, James T. Cleveland. The fact that all of Stephen's family members lived on small estates suggests that he purchased his property with his wife's inheritance.

Cleveland had lived only one year in his beautiful home before the Civil War erupted. In March 1861, he organized a company of cavalry called "The Suggsville Greys" for the Confederacy. Cleveland was the captain, his brother Alonzo was third lieutenant, and his brother Jeremiah was private. The unit was reorganized into the "Clarke County Regulars" in Memphis, Tennessee, in October 1861.

Much had changed when Cleveland returned to Suggsville. His young son, Walter, had died, and Suggsville itself was beginning to fade away. The Clarke County Agricultural Censuses indicate that in 1870, Cleveland owned 2,900 acres, which produced large quantities of corn, cotton, and sweet potatoes. However, by 1880, he had sold off most of his plantation, reducing its size to only 585 acres. He seemed to have shifted his focus to harvesting the trees on his land and cultivating his orchard of thirty peach trees. When Cleveland died in 1883, his daughter, Lillian Cleveland Dahlberg, inherited the estate. She, in turn, passed the house down to her daughter, Dora Dahlberg Young. Descendants of the Clevelands continued to own the house well into the twentieth century. A number of alterations were made in the home, including the addition of bathrooms and the cutting of doorways to allow air circulation between the rooms.

Today, the Cleveland House is used as the lodge of a private hunting club, the members of which are keeping alive the sad story of Stephen Cleveland's ghost. One of the members, Louis M. Finlay, Jr., traces the origin of the tale back to 1861. "When Stephen went off to war, his son, Walter, was asleep," he told me. "Rather than wake him up and go through a painful farewell, he rode off without saying goodbye. Walter had very hurt feelings. It took him a long time to get over it. So the next time Stephen came back, he tried to make up for it. He promised Walter that he would never leave again without telling him goodbye. He took Walter on horseback with him. The pair rode up the front steps and around the porch and then down the other steps. Of course, he was thrilled to death. He asked his father to do it over and over again. The story is told that when he came back from the war, Walter had died. This was August of 1863. Stephen was devastated by the death of his son. He was always close to Walter, probably closer than he was to his daughter. The clatter of hooves late at night and early in the morning can still be heard around the house long after Stephen's death. People say that Stephen Cleveland is taking his son, Walter, on a final ride around the porch, the ride that he was never able to take before he died."

Finlay himself is witness to one of Stephen Cleveland's late-night rides around his former home. "Many, many years ago, my wife and I and my first cousin and his wife were spending a weekend here and were playing bridge very late one night—I guess it was about one or two o'clock—when suddenly, we heard this loud clatter. It was unmistakably a clatter. It was not a possum or raccoon walking on the porch. Well, we were speechless. We sat there for a minute looking at one another. I rushed to the door and flung it open and looked out on the porch, but nothing was in sight." Of course, Finlay has not ruled out the possibility that the spectral sounds may have a rational explanation. "The house is used quite regularly by civic groups that have meetings out here. A lot of people capitalize on the story. They'll go out on the porch and make clopping sounds, like a horse is galloping on the porch, just to scare the people inside."

### The Drish House
### Tuscaloosa

Slaves built this two-story house on eighty acres of land at Seventeenth Street between Greensboro and Queen City avenues. The owner, Dr. John Drish, incorporated Greek Revival and Italianate elements in the design of his Southern colonial mansion. The brick is covered with stucco, as were many of the plantation homes in Virginia. His wife, a wealthy widow from Virginia named Mrs. McKinney, gave her husband the money for building the house. To all appearances, Dr. Drish was an attractive, well-educated physician. However, he also had a dark side. He drank to excess and gambled. Friends and relatives attributed his drinking to his huge losses at the gaming tables and to two tragedies in his life. His daughter from a previous marriage, Katherine, entered into a bad

*The Drish House was built in 1837 for John Drish, whose life was ruined by gambling and alcohol.* (Courtesy Marilyn Brown)

marriage to W. W. King after her father drove off the young man she was really in love with. After bearing two sons, she went insane, and her husband divorced her. Dr. Drish did not want his daughter committed, so he brought her back to Tuscaloosa, where she spent her time wandering around her father's plantation, accompanied by a slave woman who looked after her. Dr. Drish's niece, Helen Whiting, was also a source of great sorrow for him. She married a brutal man named Fitch, who cut her throat in a drunken rage with a straight razor. Because she was a frequent visitor to her uncle's plantation, a number of her possessions remained there after her death. The slaves soon spread the rumor that "Miss Helen'll get you if you tetch her things."

Nika McCool, a docent at the Drish House, told me that the physician's fortunes declined after the Civil War. "Prior to the Civil War, the Drishes were very wealthy. He had a quarter of a million dollars in assets. At the end of the war, they lost almost everything. His health worsened as well. Dr. Drish began drinking heavily and self-medicating with laudanum. In the parlance of the day, one report said, 'His heart was broken.' Whether he was injured or shell-shocked or stricken with a fever, we will never know. He must have known that the end was near because about a month before he died, Dr. Drish amended his will. He left the property to his wife. He also stated in the will that the children of Liza Lee [his first wife] could stay in the house." One fateful night in 1867, Dr. Drish was screaming and thrashing in bed. He escaped from the clutches of the servants who were holding him down and started running down the curved stairway. Midway down the stairs, Dr. Drish collapsed. He died soon thereafter. Dr. Drish was laid in state in the mansion's tower. Candles were placed around his coffin.

The sad house acquired a haunted reputation after Dr. Drish's death. The slaves reported hearing ghostly screams and the rush of feet during all hours of the day. No white person had ever heard sounds, even though the neighbors began talking about eerie lights coming from the tower. Mrs. Drish invited her niece, Virginia Owens Green; her husband, Thomas Finley Green; and their children to live with her. They were much better company than Katherine, who was becoming more and more withdrawn. As the years passed, Mrs. Drish began thinking about her funeral arrangements. She instructed Mrs. Green to have her coffin carried up to the tower. She also wanted her husband's funeral candles placed around her coffin. When Mrs. Drish finally died seventeen years after her husband passed away, Mrs. Green was unable to locate the candles, so the old lady was buried without them.

Not long after Mrs. Drish's death, one of the Greens' daughters sleeping alone in the downstairs bedroom had a visitor. She asked her mother why she entered her room during the night. She said that someone pulled the covers over her, turned around, and left. Her mother replied, "My dear, I didn't walk into your room last night." When it dawned on them that the girl's intruder was not human, they decided not to tell her sister. The next night, the sisters slept together, and the other girl had the same experience.

Soon, Judge W. C. Cochrane and his wife purchased the home. A sister of Mrs. Cochrane's spent the night and was visited by a ghostly intruder, just as the Greens' daughters had been. Another night, the Cochrane family was eating supper when a servant ran into the dining room, shouting, "The tower's on fire!" Judge Cochrane ran into the yard and stared at the flames coming from the tower. He returned to the house and sprinted up the stairs. The tower was completely dark.

The house was remodeled in 1887. Two more families—the Lilleys and the Snedecors—moved in after the Cochranes left. No reports of any ghostly occurrences surfaced for decades. In 1906, the Drish House was converted into the Jemison School. After the school moved into a new building, the house stood vacant for a while, incurring substantial damage from vandalism and neglect. The Tuscaloosa Wrecking Company leased the house in the 1930s. The owners repaired the roof, replaced the broken windows, and erected a fence around the building. In 1940, the school district sold the house to the Southside Baptist Church, which attached additions to the old building. By the 1990s, the church was making plans to demolish the building, which was, once again, in a sad state of disrepair. In 1994, the Heritage Commission of Tuscaloosa intervened, saving the Drish mansion. With the help of the Tuscaloosa Preservation Society, the commission painted the building and made other improvements. The additions to the building have been removed, restoring much of its nineteenth-century grandeur.

Today, the Drish House is rented out for special events, such as weddings and receptions. According to Nika McCool, paranormal groups have taken a strong interest in the historic home. She remains skeptical about otherworldly presences in the house, although she admits that the sweet fragrance of perfume occasionally wafts through.

On October 6 and 16, 2008, the Tuscaloosa Paranormal Research Group investigated the Drish House. They collected a number of intriguing electronic voice phenomena (EVPs) on the first and second floor, including: "That way," "Hey, Mike!" "Thank you," "My thing's in there," and "Help me!" On October 16, the group set up a forty-channel DVR system with infrared cameras in a second-floor room where they had collected evidence earlier. A toy piano was set up in the middle. When one of the members asked questions, the piano began playing on its own. It was so loud that members on the first floor heard it. Could it be that the spirits of the women of the Drish House are trying to entertain their guests with their piano playing?

## The Dunning House
## Thomasville

The Dunning House was built by George Dunning in 1897. He was an entrepreneur who once owned several businesses in Thomasville, including a livery stable and a theater. Linda Vice, the current owner, was told by people who knew the Dunning family that even though George was proud of his fine home, he did not really enjoy entertaining there. She said that the house passed into the Lowery family after one of the Dunnings' daughters married one of "Granny" Lowery's sons. "[The Lowerys'] son and daughter took possession of it and rented out the upstairs during World War II. After the war, it was used as a home for the mill [sawmill] managers. I moved into the house in 1975." Linda felt that she belonged there after discovering that her great-great-grandfather was the contractor for the house.

Linda named her home "The Enchanted Cottage" after making the acquaintance of its first occupant. She sensed that she was not the only one in the house when doors that she had locked stood open the next morning. "Many times, I have found the doors open about three inches," Linda told me. She has seen George, but only out of the corner of her eye: "George walks through the dining room to the living room. He peeks into the living room and then moves on." Interestingly enough, George now seems to like company: "A number of people who have come to visit have glimpsed him. He is always dressed up. He was a very good-looking, tall man with black hair and roses in his cheeks." George's appearance made such an impression on her that when two of his grandsons came to visit, she immediately recognized them as members of the Dunning family. "One was tall and one was short. They both looked like George Dunning. Later, we had a Dunning family reunion at my house."

George Dunning is not the only ghost in Linda's home. "Mr. George had a number of children. One of them was a hydrocephalic child, and he was kept upstairs. The guests who have seen him say that he is not as welcoming as Mr. George. He had a habit of coming into people's rooms at night and looking at them in bed. When I had the upstairs renovated, he disappeared."

The Enchanted Cottage's third ghost is not a member of the Dunning family: "I have a friend from Mobile who is a psychic. She even works with the FBI on hard-to-solve cases. One day, while she was visiting me, she walked into the living room and saw a little old lady sitting in a chair, reading a Bible. I asked a couple of people about [the ghost], and they said it was probably Granny Lowery. She was a Holiness—a Pentecostal. She was a small woman, and she wore her hair in a little topknot."

In the decades that Linda Vice has lived in the Dunning House, she has never really been frightened of her resident ghost. To say that she has learned to live with her ghost would be an understatement: "So many people have seen George that it's become kind of a joke when something weird happens—'Well, there's George again.'"

## Gaineswood
## Demopolis

Demopolis was founded in 1817. One of the town's first citizens was Nathan Bryan Whitfield. Born in Lenoir County, North Carolina, in 1799, he soon proved to be a child prodigy. He was admitted into the University of North Carolina at the age of twelve and graduated at the age of seventeen. Whitfield went on to attend graduate school at the University of Chapel Hill. In February 1819, he married his cousin Elizabeth Watkins Whitfield. While living in North Carolina, the couple became the parents of four children, three of whom died young. After being appointed director of the Bank of Newbern, North Carolina, in 1832, Whitfield became interested in the rich, cotton-producing land of Marengo County in Alabama's Black Belt.

In 1834, after serving in the House of Commons and the state senate and being promoted to the rank of major general in the state militia, Whitfield and his family moved to West Alabama. Whitfield later moved to 4,000 acres of land he purchased in 1837. The plantation, which he called Chatham, was located near the town of Jefferson. During their time there, several more children were born. By 1842, the Whitfields had become the parents of three living daughters and four living sons. That same year, though, three of the children died within five weeks. Convinced that Chatham was an unhealthy environment, Whitfield purchased the property on which Gaineswood now stands. The first documented owner was George Strother Gaines, who built a dogtrot cabin on the site. Gaines had used the structure as his home and office. During most of the 1820s, he and a local businessman traded with the Choctaws out of this cabin. As a U.S. Indian agent, Gaines met with Pushmataha, chief of the

Choctaws, and negotiated the treaty under an oak tree that resulted in the removal of his people to the Indian Territory. This historic tree became known throughout the region as the Pushmataha Oak. Gaines moved to Mobile before selling the property to Whitfield.

Between 1843 and 1861, Whitfield transformed the cabin into one of the showplaces of the Black Belt. His wife, Elizabeth, died in 1846, fifteen years before the beautiful home she and Nathan had dreamed of was completed. In 1843, Whitfield named the estate Marlmont, but he renamed it Gaineswood in honor of George Strother Gaines. After reading Stuart and Revett's *The Antiquities of Athens and Other Monuments of Greece* (1837) and Minard Lafever's *The Modern Builder's Guide* (1833) and *The Beauties of Modern Architecture* (1835), Whitfield decided to incorporate elements from several architectural styles. The exterior of the brick-and-stucco mansion features eighteen fluted Doric columns, as well as fourteen plain square pillars that support the porches. The two fluted columns

*Construction of Gaineswood was completed in 1861. The owner, Nathan Bryan Whitfield, named his mansion after Indian agent George Strother Gaines.* (Photo from en.wikipedia.org)

in the entranceway reflect the Ionic style. The four Corinthian columns in the ballroom are lined with vis-à-vis (facing) mirrors. The ballroom also includes twenty-four Corinthian pilasters, a coffered ceiling, and a beautiful plaster cornice. In the master's bedroom, two fluted Ionic columns support a cornice; two fluted Corinthian columns front a bay window in the mistress's bedroom. Stained-glass transom panels depict scenes from mythology. The workmen brought to Demopolis from Philadelphia created the fresco and panel painting inside the house. Most of the construction, however, was the product of slave labor.

The grounds of Gaineswood are preserved in a steel engraving created by artist John Sartain at the time the Whitfields lived there. In the foreground is an artificial lake, with paths landscaped around its circumference. Several of the outbuildings depicted in the engraving, including the slave quarters, kitchen, and stables, are still standing. When the lake was filled in, the gazebo was moved closer to the house. Between 1845 and 1863, Whitfield's slaves dug a drainage canal to divert the estate's rainfall into the Tombigbee River. The canal is one mile long and thirty feet deep.

Gaineswood suffered very little damage during the Civil War. In 1862, Whitfield was walking across a bridge near his canal when a plank broke, causing him to fall. He severely injured his leg and walked with a noticeable limp throughout the remainder of his life. His health declined as well. He was so weak that he had difficulty signing his name three years later. Before Whitfield died in 1868, he sold the estate to his son, Bryan Watkins Whitfield. Whitfield's daughter Edith bought Gaineswood in 1896. The Whitfields continued living in the house until it was purchased by the Kirven family in 1923. Several other people owned Gaineswood before it was sold to the state of Alabama in 1967. After Gaineswood was restored, the Alabama Historical Commission (AHC) acquired it. In 1973, Gaineswood was designated as a National Historic Landmark. The Friends of Gaineswood, a support group comprised of Whitfield's descendants and local civic leaders, are active partners with the AHC in site preservation.

Gaineswood was opened to the public in 1975. Docents begin their tours of the historic home by pointing out the portrait of Whitfield's daughter Edith in the parlor. They also call attention to the flutina, a sort of player piano, and a music box, both of which he designed. Whitfield's legacy is preserved as well in Gaineswood's ghost stories, not all of which have been "debunked."

Nathan Bryan Whitfield is a key player in Gaineswood's signature ghost story, made famous in Kathryn Tucker Windham's 1969 book *13 Alabama Ghosts and Jeffrey.* The story goes that after the death of Elizabeth Whitfield in 1846, her husband hired a Miss Carter to help with the household chores and take care of the younger children. Because Miss Carter's family lived in Virginia, she soon became homesick. Whitfield took note of the young woman's depression and invited her sister, Evelyn, to spend the winter at Gaineswood. She proved to be a delightful addition to the general's family. On cold winter evenings, Whitfield played martial tunes on the bagpipes, and Evelyn accompanied him on the piano. The once gloomy house was transformed by her presence into a place of joy.

Unfortunately, the happy times at Gaineswood were cut short by Evelyn's untimely death. No one knows for certain why the young woman died. Some say that she developed pneumonia from inhaling the cold, damp air of Marengo County. Others say that her death was precipitated by her ill-fated romance with a handsome young French count. He had traveled to Marengo County to visit relatives who were part of Napoleon's Vine and Olive Colony. The couple fell in love and became engaged. One afternoon, Evelyn and the count had an argument, and, in a fit of rage, he removed the engagement ring from her finger and tossed it into the bushes. He left Marengo County, never to return, and Evelyn died soon thereafter, perhaps of a broken heart.

Following Evelyn's death, Whitfield was presented with a dilemma. He had promised the girl on her deathbed that she would be buried in the family plot in Virginia. However, at the time of her death, the roads were caked with ice, snow, and mud, making them impassable. He could not return her body to Virginia by train because the railroad did not arrive in Marengo County until 1862. Left with no alternative, Whitfield had Evelyn's corpse placed in a coffin, which was sealed with resin and stored temporarily in the cellar under the stairs. A few days later, members of the Whitfield household began hearing footsteps coming up the cellar stairs and proceeding to the drawing room, where the piano stood. Late at night, people were awakened by the sound of Scottish ballads being played on a piano. The music stopped playing when the listener went down to the cellar to investigate the source of the sound. The disturbances ceased temporarily after the roads dried up and Evelyn's coffin was finally carried home. However, members of the Whitfield family continually heard the spectral sounds well into the twentieth century.

As the docents at Gaineswood point out, Ms. Windham's account should be taken as folklore and not as historical fact. According to the family letters, Whitfield was reluctant to send his daughters Edith and Betsy to any of the region's private schools, including Judson Female Institute and Demopolis Female Academy. Instead, he hired a teacher, Elizabeth Robertson, and a governess, Elizabeth's sister Charlotte, to educate the girls at home in the mid-1850s. However, not long after Elizabeth arrived at Gaineswood, her health began to deteriorate. One day, she had a seizure so severe that Whitfield called for his son, Dr. Bryan Watkins Whitfield. On May 5, 1856, Dr. Whitfield revived Elizabeth by applying artificial respiration, but she died in an upstairs bedroom on May 15. Her remains were placed in the Glover Mausoleum for a few months before being transported to her family in New York. General Whitfield traveled to New York and met Elizabeth's coffin at the train station. Just prior to his arrival in New York, he had attended the inauguration of Pres. James Buchanan in Washington, D.C. He later enrolled Edith and Betsy in a boarding school.

Not surprisingly, the true story is far less romantic than the legend. However, in recent years, a number of reports of ghostly activity at Gaineswood have surfaced. In 1999, this writer interviewed an elderly resident of Demopolis who said that she had a sleepover at Gaineswood during World War I and was awakened by the sound of

*Mirrors give the grand ballroom at Gaineswood the illusion of depth. Guests spending the night have had their sleep interrupted by ghostly piano playing.* (Photo from Wikimedia Commons)

someone playing Stephen Foster songs on the piano. She ran down the stairs and was surprised to find that the drawing room was empty.

According to Paige Smith and Linda Ray, two of the docents at Gaineswood, a number of unexplained occurrences have taken place while they were working there. Linda told me that one day, a visitor who claimed to have psychic abilities felt three different presences in the house. During a tour of the home, she said that she sensed the spirit of a woman walking between the boys' bedroom and the room next to it.

Paige told me about an experience she had in the house in June 2015. "I was getting ready to lock up. I turned off the lights upstairs. I came downstairs and I smelled this really sweet smell that smelled like gardenias. I thought, 'O.K. That was odd.' I didn't say anything about it. A couple of weeks later, the same thing happened again in the same spot. So I went upstairs the second time and said, 'Linda, have you ever smelled gardenias between the parlor and the dining room?' She said no. I said, 'Well, come down here so you can smell it too.' She couldn't smell it. I told the director about it, and she said, 'I know what it is. It's the air freshener I put in here.' I looked at it and said, 'That's purple. That's not it. That's lavender.'"

Paige's son began working at Gaineswood on May 6, 2016, as the groundskeeper. "He came down the steps," she recalled. "I was working in the gift shop. He said, 'Mama, come here a minute.' He was standing in the place where I smelled the gardenias. He said, 'Do you smell flowers?' I said, 'Our ghost is welcoming you.' He said, 'What?' We have had three people here who sense something when they get to this point. We don't know who it is. My son said, 'The only way I can describe it is it smells pink.' I said, 'O.K.' When we got home that night, he said, 'This is going to sound weird, but I get this vibe that it's a girl in her mid-twenties to mid-thirties.' I said, 'O.K.' He's an English major, and he has a vivid imagination, but still, what he said was pretty weird."

Linda's experience with Gaineswood's ghost happened on the same day as Paige's son's. "I was standing right here [between the parlor and the dining room], and I smelled it too. It wasn't the air freshener."

A talkative psychic who toured the house in March 2012 gave the docents information about Gaineswood's ghosts that put their minds at ease. "When we got to the hall, he started walking back and forth while I was trying to tell him about the vis-à-vis mirrors," Paige said. "When he reached the portraits of Bryan Watkins Whitfield and his wife, he turned to me and said, 'Do you know that they're still here?' I said, 'O.K.' He said, "Their eyes follow you. If a portrait's eyes follow you, that means their spirit is still here.' He said that he had a house in Missouri, and a psychic came in and told him what to look for if he wanted to know whether or not a house is haunted. The man walked around the house [Gaineswood] and said, 'All the other rooms are peaceful. [She pointed to the portraits.] These are the only two spirits who are still here.' I told the man, 'You might think I'm an idiot, but every night when I turn off the lights, I say goodnight to everybody.' He said, 'They know that you respect them and that you care about the house. You will always be welcome here.'"

## Jemison-Van de Graaff Mansion
## Tuscaloosa

In the mid-nineteenth century, Robert Jemison, Jr. (1802-71), was known as one of Alabama's most successful entrepreneurs. He earned a fortune as an operator of toll roads and a stage line and as the owner of a foundry and surface coalmines. Jemison also owned six plantations and over five hundred slaves, many of whom acquired marketable skills while in his service. As state senator, he voted against secession at the Secession Conference in Montgomery in 1861. However, after Alabama seceded from the Union on January 11, 1861, Jemison remained loyal to his state, serving in the Confederate Senate from 1863 to 1865.

Despite his immense wealth and power, Jemison frequently found himself on the brink of bankruptcy. In 1858, he put up for sale his six plantations, seventy slaves, a livery stable, a private residence, and the Indian Queen Hotel. However, within a few months, Jemison recovered financially and did not have to sell his property. After the Civil War, Jemison campaigned for the building of a hospital for the mentally ill. He also participated in the rebuilding of the University of Alabama.

In 1859, after having saved his fortune, Jemison began making plans to build a grand house on Market Street, now Greensboro Avenue. He hired a Philadelphia architect named Samuel Sloan to design the home. Sloan's partner, John Stewart, was completing the construction of the Alabama Insane Hospital (now Bryce Hospital) when he was asked to supervise the building of Jemison's mansion.

Most of the Italianate mansion was completed by 1862, although the family did not move into the house until 1863. The exterior clearly reflects Stewart's intention to create a mansion that would become one of the showplaces of the South. The ornate wraparound porch is festooned with arches and columns. He also incorporated cutting-edge technology into the mansion. Water collected in the gutters was directed into pipes in the wall. The water then ran outside through brick pipes and was collected in three huge brick-

*The Jemison-Van de Graaff Mansion was built in 1862.* (Photo from Wikimedia Commons)

and-cement cisterns. A slave waiting in the basement pumped the water into wooden tanks in the attic.

The twenty-six-room mansion also had a gas stove and a dry well in the basement, which kept food cool and fresh because the temperature stayed at a constant fifty degrees. One of the mansion's most innovative features was its indoor lighting fueled by coal gas produced by a coal gas plant on the property. Some of Stewart's plans, such as a central heating plant, never came to fruition because of the Yankee blockade. Jemison used the mansion primarily as his townhouse. It cost $80,000 to build, the equivalent of $2.2 million today.

In 1865, the Jemison house narrowly avoided being burned by the Union Army. One legend has it that when the Union Army reached Tuscaloosa, the soldiers were under orders to arrest Jemison because he was a Confederate senator. Jemison learned of the Union authorities' plan and hid out in the swamps. When the Yankees arrived at the Jemison mansion, his wife, Priscilla Cherokee (Taylor) Jemison, was given fifteen minutes to collect her things and leave.

*Robert Jemison, Jr., an entrepreneur and state senator, built his grand home in Tuscaloosa as a townhouse.* (Courtesy Marilyn Brown)

Suddenly, a group of boys came running down the street exclaiming, "Forrest is coming! Forrest is coming!" The soldiers left quickly without inflicting any serious damage on the house.

Following Jemison's death in 1871, the home remained in the family well into the twentieth century. Jemison's most famous descendant is Robert Jemison Van de Graaff, who is remembered today as the inventor of the high-voltage Van de Graaff generator. In the 1940s, J. P. and Neil Burchfield purchased and renovated the mansion. Between 1955 and 1979, the historic home housed the Friedman Public Library. For a brief time, two local publications—*Horizon* and *Antique Monthly*—had offices inside the mansion. The Jemison-Van de Graaff Mansion Foundation acquired the property in 1991, which restored the mansion to its original appearance. Today, the mansion serves as a house museum and events venue. The Tuscaloosa Convention and Visitors Bureau occupies the lower levels. The beautiful furnishings and craftsmanship that make the old home an ideal setting for weddings and other social gatherings mask the tragic events that still resonate in the mansion's ghost stories.

Stories of ghostly presences surfaced not long after the mansion was opened to the general public. Visitors and staff reported hearing disembodied voices, usually at night. Some people walking through the house felt as if they were being watched by unseen eyes. Objects that were placed in one part of the mansion before closing time were discovered in an entirely different spot the next morning. Staff members who thought they were alone in the house were surprised to hear music and heavy footsteps. A number of people have heard a loud crashing sound, like a china cabinet falling over. The source of the sound has never been found. The figure of a small girl in nineteenth-century garb has been seen standing on the grand staircase. The most dramatic paranormal incident occurred when a bride was in one of the rooms preparing for her wedding at the mansion. Without warning, a large mirror flew across the room. When the young woman regained her composure, she said that it looked as if someone had thrown the mirror.

*Docents have heard heavy footsteps and music playing in the Jemison-Van de Graaff Mansion when they thought they were alone.* (Courtesy Marilyn Brown)

This writer and his wife, Marilyn, took a tour of the Jemison-Van de Graaff Mansion in July 2016. We walked up the stairs with the rest of the group. After several minutes, both Marilyn and I were short of breath. Walking up the stairs was not tiring at all, so we have no explanation for our breathing problems, which lasted only a minute or so.

Much of the ghostly activity that has been reported in the Jemison mansion over the years can be traced back to Robert Jemison's daughter, Cherokee. In 1865, Cherokee married a young lawyer from Tuscaloosa named Andrew Coleman Hargrove. A veteran of the Civil War, Hargrove was shot in head during the Battle of Nashville. The bullet entered Hargrove's skull in front of the ear and lodged in his brain. As a result, he suffered from headaches for the rest of his life. Despite his injury, Hargrove had a distinguished career as a state senator, land commissioner, and professor of law at the University of Alabama. In December 1895, after enduring more than thirty years of agony, Hargrove shot himself in library of the Jemison home. His widow, Cherokee, sank into a deep depression from which she never recovered. In a letter written in January 1900, her son-in-law said that she often became "wild with hysteria" and worried about "small things of no real importance." She passed away on May 4, 1903, but she and her husband live on in the tales that people still tell about the Jemison-Van de Graaff Mansion.

## Kendall Manor
### Eufaula

Kendall Manor was built in 1850 in the Italianate style by architect H. George Whipple. The owner of the house, James Turner Kendall, was a wealthy cotton factor. Kendall Manor is a standout among Eufaula's more than seven hundred homes because of the distinctive white belvedere, or tower, that crowns the two-story structure. Kendall Manor is also distinctive because of its haunted past.

When the home was built, the slaves told the story of a man on a white horse who appeared only when something bad was about to happen. Kendall's children scoffed at this story until Kendall's manservant, Logan, saw a tall man wearing a gray uniform and a broad-brimmed hat ride past the house. The next day, James Turner Kendall died.

The ghost of a nursemaid to the Kendall children also haunts the old mansion. Two of the former owners of Kendall Manor, Timothy and Barbara Lubsend, said that when Annie the nursemaid was around, no one could get away with anything. One of the great-great-great-grandsons of James Turner Kendall had a personal encounter with Annie while he and his brothers were racing around the veranda on their tricycles. The youngest boy glanced up at the dining-room window and saw Annie standing there with her hands on her hips. She was wearing her black dress and starched apron. The boy was so frightened that he lost control of his tricycle and fell off.

*A ghostly nursemaid named Annie walks the halls of Kendall Manor in her black dress and starched apron.* (Courtesy Wikimedia Commons)

He suffered scrapes and bruises, but at least he did not race around the veranda anymore. In fact, even as an adult, he would not go near the dining-room window.

After Kendall Manor became a bed-and-breakfast, guests reported seeing several other apparitions as well, including a woman wearing a Victorian-era dress and a little girl on the porch. The identity of these spirits is unknown. However, the man wearing a top hat who has been seen in the parlor bears a resemblance to James Turner Kendall. Today, Kendall Manor is a private residence.

### Lakewood
### Livingston

Built in 1832 by Joseph Lake, Lakewood is located off Washington

Street across the street from the University of West Alabama. Unlike most antebellum homes in Alabama, Lakewood has been owned and occupied by seven members of the same family. Its most famous "guest" was educator and social reformer Julia Tutwiler, who served as president of the university from 1881 to 1910. Today, Lakewood is owned by Olivia "Sweetie Pie" Collins.

According to Sweetie Pie, Lakewood has always had a ghost. Longtime area resident Eloise Boyd told me that she saw him twice while she was visiting there in the 1940s. She was sitting in the kitchen one morning eating breakfast when she observed a man walk past the window. Bradford Jones, the grandson of the owners, told her that she had just seen the ghost. On a second visit, she was spending the night when she noticed a man walking down the drive between the big house and the guesthouse. He seemed to be wearing a work shirt. Once again, Jones identified the strange man as Lakewood's resident ghost.

*Sightings of a man in a work shirt have been reported for years at Lakewood.* (Photo by Alan Brown)

Over twenty years later, Bradford Jones' daughter, Sweetie Pie, first saw the ghost when she was in college. "I was on the third floor," she told me. "I was the only one on 'The Hill.' (We call the big house 'The Hill.') We had rented the third floor to a friend of mine from college. I went up to change the bed when, out of the corner of my eye, I saw a man in a plaid shirt walk by. I said, 'Oh, you scared me!' I thought it was my uncle. He had a shirt that looked just like it. But when I looked outside of the room, there was no one there. I went and sat outside until my daddy came home. My daddy—his name was Bradford Jones—said, 'What's the matter with you? What are you doing out here?' I said I wasn't going back there with that ghost walking around. From then on, I would never go on the third floor." She has not seen the apparition since that day.

Most witnesses, however, say that the ghost appeared to them as a wispy image, something resembling a white shirt. Sweetie Pie's family members have gotten used to sharing their home with the white apparition, with the exception of her daughter, Sydney, who does not share her mother's and grandfather's view of the ghost as a benign entity. "Sydney is scared to death of it," Sweetie Pie said. "She will not go in the big house by herself."

Some of Sydney's friends have also had "spooky" experiences inside Lakewood. One afternoon in 2009, a friend from school named Tyler stopped by to shower after football practice. "I was just showering, and nobody was here," he said. "The lights flicked off, and I didn't think anything of it. I figured it was somebody just playing a joke on me." Tyler became increasingly concerned, however, when the light flicked on and off several times. He climbed out of the shower and got dressed as fast as he could. He then waited outside until a member of the family returned home.

Another guest had an even more terrifying experience inside the house. She was sleeping in a downstairs room when she sensed that something else was there. When her eyes became acclimated to the dark, the woman clearly saw someone sitting on the side of the bed. A child and a woman were standing against a wall. The strange night visitors vanished in a few seconds.

Sweetie Pie believes she knows the identity of the ghost haunting the guesthouse. The original guesthouse was converted from a chicken coop. After being demolished by Hurricane Ivan, the guesthouse was rebuilt. Sweetie Pie had her second encounter with the paranormal on the porch. "I have had a spirit on the front porch in that rocking chair right outside the window," she said. She believes that the spirit of her mother, who lived in the guesthouse before she died, is rocking the chair.

In the last week of October 2009, this writer visited Lakewood, along with two staff members from the *Meridian Star:* Jennifer Brown, reporter, and Paula Merritt, photographer. We were standing outside the guesthouse, listening to Sweetie Pie talk about the front porch, when suddenly, the rocking chair started rocking. The wind was not blowing at the time. Then we walked over to the front of the big house to take photographs. This seemingly simple task turned out to be very challenging. Every time Paula snapped the shutter, the camera would take two photographs. She shot a number of pictures of the front of the home, many of which had orbs in them. As we were walking back to our cars, Paula said that in her twenty-five years working as a newspaper photographer, she had never had anything like this happen before,

Living with a ghost tends to make life unpredictable. However, having a spirit in the house can also be comforting. Even when she was little, Sweetie Pie felt that the ghost was a friendly spirit, a sort of family protector. "I was never afraid of him. He was a part of us. He's just the caretaker, our spirit that's floating by and doesn't let anything bad happen here."

## Oakhurst
## Emelle

Oakhurst is one of three homes built by members of the Winston family. It was built in the Hamner-Sumterville area in 1854 by Augustus Anthony Winston (1815-97) as a summer retreat. Oak Hill was built six miles away by his brother, William Overton Winston (1809-94). A third brother, James McDonald Winston (1826-1905), built a large home in Sumter County called Oak Lawn. Their first cousin, John Al Winston, built a house between Gainesville and Emelle. He served as governor of Alabama from 1853 to 1857. John A. Winston has the distinction of being the first native-born governor of the state. He is buried in Winston Cemetery.

Oakhurst was built on a small knoll on Gainesville-Lacy's Ford Road, approximately eight miles from Gainesville. The two-story, Greek Revival structure has a low hipped roof encircled by a bracketed cornices. On the north end of the house are two chimneys. A one-story porch with a low hipped roof is supported by six square wooden columns with a wheat-sheaf balustrade. The four-paneled main-entry doors with sidelights and transoms are original to the house. All of the woodwork in the interior is original as well, including the baseboards, Lafeveresque architraves with cornices, a dogleg staircase in the entry hall, and random-width heart-pine flooring. The only alterations to the house are the brick infill between the original brick foundation piers and the partial enclosure of the back porch.

Retired librarian McGregor Smith is the great-granddaughter of Augustus Anthony Winston, the builder of Oakhurst. She told me that as she was growing up in the house, she expected to see the ghosts of slaves who had lived and worked there in the nineteenth century. She did not have proof that the house was haunted until years after she was married. One night, while her brother-in-law, Pat, lay dying in his hospital bed in Fairhope, she and her family returned to Oakhurst. They were sitting in the living room, drinking coffee, when they heard low whispers in an upstairs bedroom. She thought that her daughter was up in her room, so she called to her to turn off the light. After a couple of minutes, McGregor's husband, Tip, went upstairs to check on her, but the room was empty.

After a while, the strange incident faded from McGregor's memory. Then two weeks later, she and her oldest daughter went to the doctor in Meridian to see if a growth she had was malignant. After the doctor took a few tests, the women returned home, concerned about what the tests might reveal. "We were sitting in the living room when we heard the voices again. My daughter said, 'That radio's on upstairs.' But there was no one there just like last time. I think this was Pat's way of telling us not to grieve over losing him because he would always be with us, in one way or another."

McGregor Smith's daughter, Janie Wooldridge, lives in Oakhurst with her husband, Brett. For Janie, Oakhurst is the family home, a place of warm memories and good times. Still, at times, Oakhurst takes on an entirely different dimension. "There aren't any really great stories," Janie told me. "It's more like little things we've heard and seen. We've heard music. In fact, I got up in the middle of the night one night and heard what sounded like harpsichord music. At first, I thought one of the cats had brushed up against one of Brett's guitars. I walked into the room where I heard it, and the music continued to play. Then all of a sudden, it just stopped."

Spectral voices still resound through the halls of Oakhurst as well. "My mother and I both heard a voice calling the name of a dog I had at that time—Katie," Janie said. "Of course, we hear bumps and things all the time. My mother and I heard distant voices in another room talking. One night, we had just found out that my father's brother had died and [we had] been to town to see Louis [Smith, her grandfather], and when we got back, my mother and I had stayed downstairs and were sitting up talking, and we heard these distant voices. We couldn't make out what they were saying. It was just like a roomful of people talking."

In recent years, a full-body apparition has appeared in Oakhurst. "Now Brett has actually seen things," Janie said. "He'll be sitting in a chair and see somebody. In fact, he identified one of them. I got out some old pictures, and we think it was my great-great-grandfather."

Despite those startling moments that interrupt the Wooldridges' routine, Janie is not really afraid of the spirits. "I think the ghosts are friendly," she said. "I know they tend to appear more when there's something going on. Like once, I was refinishing floors in half of the house, and I had just moved the furniture into the other half of the house, and we saw a lot of activity then. Also, when we were building

*The full-body apparition of Augustus Anthony Winston haunts the halls of Oakhurst.* (Courtesy Sumter County Historical Society)

the swimming pool, there was a lot going on. We also used to see a lot of activity from October to December, but lately, we haven't had any activity at all. I haven't really made any alterations to the house lately." Most likely, Oakhurst's ghosts will remain dormant until Janie decides to make more home improvements.

## Oakleigh
## Mobile

James W. Roper was a brick mason, cotton factor, and dry-goods merchant. His Water Street brickyard was located where the RSA Battle House Tower now stands. In 1833, he designed and built his *T*-shaped Greek Revival mansion on thirty-five acres of land west of Mobile. The house was constructed primarily by slave and free labor. The bricks came from a clay pit on the property. The timber on his land provided the lumber. Roper was attracted to the site because of the majestic oak trees on the property. In fact, the mansion's name, Oakleigh, is a combination of the words "oak" and "lea," another word for "meadow." Oakleigh is noteworthy for its grand double parlors, cantilevered front staircase, and six-over-six windows and galleries. Because he and his wife, Margaret, planned to hold lavish parties at their home, Roper added a north hallway to accommodate the double parlors on the south side of the house. During the construction of the mansion, Roper's wife and first child died. His life took another downturn during the Panic of 1837. when he found himself unable to repay the $200,000 loan he had taken out to build his home. After the bank repossessed the house, Roper's brother-in-law bought it, along with half of the acreage and seventeen of Roper's eighteen slaves. He then gave Roper and his family permission to live there rent free. Roper remarried in 1838 and had four children with his second wife, Eliza Ann Simison. Roper salvaged part of his fortune by becoming a lumber merchant. He and his family moved to New Orleans in 1850.

Alfred Irwin, a treasurer of the Mobile and Ohio Railroad, became

*James W. Roper built this mansion in 1833. Its name, "Oakleigh," is a combination of the words "oak" and "lea," which is another word for "meadow."* (Photo from en.wikipedia.org)

the next owner of Oakleigh in 1852. His wife, Margaret Kilshaw Irwin, was born in Britain. According to legend, she prevented the Union Army from destroying the mansion by hanging the Union Jack from the front gallery and declaring the estate as neutral territory. Because of Mrs. Irwin's act of defiance, she and her husband retained possession of their home throughout the war. The Irwin family prospered in the second half of the nineteenth century. Alfred and Margaret's two sons, T.K. and Lee Fearn Irwin, also achieved positions of prominence in Mobile. T.K. served as president of the Mobile Cotton Exchange. Lee became president of the Cherokee Cotton Mills, manager of Mobile Oil Mills, and assistant postmaster. During the 1870s, the parties hosted by T.K.'s socialite wife, Mary Irwin, were among Mobile's most prestigious social events, attended by politicians, artists, writers, and actors. Mary and T.K. put their own stamp on the mansion, adding a bathroom and west wing. Mary Irwin died in 1907; T.K. Irwin died in 1911. By the time their daughter, Daisy Irwin Clisby, sold the family mansion in 1916, it was known as the "Irwin Place." The new owners, Dr. and Mrs. Herbert Cole, decided to renovate the interior of the house after repairing hurricane damage to the exterior.

According to Elizabeth Parker, author of *Mobile Ghosts: Alabama's Haunted Port City*, a number of sightings have been reported in the upstairs second parlor over the years. A docent working in the guide's room downstairs heard someone walking across the second parlor when she was alone. Another docent was passing the second parlor early one morning when she noticed that the two armchairs facing the fireplace had been turned the other way. A tour group walking through the room was surprised to see the heavy chandelier vibrate. The cause was never determined. Another tour group in the second parlor heard disembodied voices coming from the library, which was unoccupied. Cameras have been known to malfunction in the bedroom as well.

Other parts of the second floor are also haunted. The shadow of a long skirt has been seen on the door of the Baitre bedroom. Visitors have seen the apparition of a woman in a white dress in the upstairs hallway.

Barbara Flannigan, a docent at Oakleigh, told me that although she has never had a personal encounter with the spirits of Oakleigh, she finds the stories she has heard to be intriguing. She mentioned the tale of the little boy who refused to enter the back parlor with the rest of his tour group because he sensed the presence of an evil woman in the room. Another docent told her that she was giving a tour in T.K. Irwin's bedroom, and they all heard the lilting sound of music. She said it sounded as though it was coming from a music box, but there was none in the room at the time.

The incident that really captured Barbara's imagination occurred on July 28, 2016. "A man spent the night here who worked for the New York City Landmarks Preservation Commission. He visits a lot of old houses. He presents workshops, where he asks people who have toured the homes what they liked the best and what they disliked the most about these places. Then he writes articles about the house. He said that at 2:00 A.M., he heard voices, things shifting

*A small boy refused to enter the back parlor of Oakleigh because he sensed an evil presence in the room.* (Courtesy Marilyn Brown)

around, and people walking through the house. He has stayed the night at a lot of old homes, and nothing has happened. He was so scared at Oakleigh that he had to take something to help him get back to sleep."

Only a few groups have stayed at Oakleigh after hours. Barbara mentioned the experience of a former member of the Oakleigh Belles, a group of high-school girls who give tours dressed in antebellum costume. "One of the girls is now the director of the Oakleigh Belles. She said that her first year here, she and the other girls were spending the night at Oakleigh for an event the next day. Late in the evening, she heard music playing upstairs. The other girls in the group heard it too. She walked up the stairs to investigate, but the floor was empty."

Paranormal groups have had bizarre encounters in Oakleigh. The members of one group reported smelling kerosene on their hands. Another group, Ghost Hunters of the South, filmed the doors of a brandy closet swinging open, almost striking a member of the group. An investigator tried to recreate the event but was unsuccessful. Another member of the group recorded a distinctly audible male voice. Later that night, an investigator was standing outside by a well when his equipment flew out of his hands and smashed on the top of the well. He said it seemed as if it had been thrown by a disembodied hand.

Even though Barbara Flannigan is a trained historian, she is open to the possibility that Oakleigh really is haunted. "A lot of people died here of natural causes, so I guess their spirits could still be in the house. Nothing has happened that I can't explain. Part of me wishes I did have something weird happen, but at the same time, I am a scaredy-cat. I don't know if I could handle the ghosts."

## Richards DAR House
## Mobile

The Richards DAR House was built by a steamboat captain from Maine. Charles G. Richards married Caroline Elizabeth Steele in 1842. Before long, the itinerant life of a steamboat captain became less and less attractive, so he decided to try his hand as a merchant in the port city of Mobile. In 1859, Charles and Caroline decided to begin construction on a house large enough to accommodate their growing family. They moved into their downtown mansion in 1860. After giving birth to her eleventh child, Caroline died in 1862. Captain Richards remained a widower for the rest of his life. He was never lonesome, though, because of all the children in the house. The mansion remained in the Richards family until 1946, when it was purchased by the Ideal Cement Company. Intent on preserving the historical integrity of the home, the owners spent thousands of dollars restoring it. In 1973, Ideal Cement donated the house to the city of Mobile. The Richards House eventually became the headquarters of the Daughters of the American Revolution (DAR), which converted it into a museum. The DAR also rents out the mansion for wedding receptions and gives tours of the home daily.

People have been talking about the ghosts inside the Richards DAR House since it was opened to the public. Docents began sharing tales about hearing strange sounds, such as disembodied voices coming from upstairs room. Many people have reported hearing faint whispers and the boisterous laughter of children around the top of the stairs. Interestingly enough, this was the favorite play area for the Richardses' children.

A docent named Mary Ruth Andrews talked to me about the experience another tour guide had inside the house around 2013. "The tour guide had just come in the house. She turned on the lights and was getting ready for the first tour of the day. She walked into one of the parlors on the first floor, and when she looked in the mirror, she saw a man sitting on a sofa where the chair is now. Now, she was confused because she had just opened the house. She hadn't unlocked the front door—just the back door. By the time it sank in that there was a man in the house who didn't belong there, she turned around to ask him who he was, and he wasn't there. She said that she had seen him very clearly."

Andrews has had only one experience in the house that might be considered paranormal. "One night, I was closing up. I walked into a

*The Richards DAR House was built by former steamboat captain Charles Richards for his wife and their eleven children. It was renovated by the Ideal Cement Company in 1946.* (Photo from Wikimedia Commons)

room, and I heard a loud bang behind me. I thought, 'What in the world was that?' So I turned around, and there was a candle that had fallen over on top of a table. A candle does not make that kind of sound."

Before long, visitors began having strange experiences as well. A docent named Debbie McShane told me that in 2015, a special event was held on the first floor. Suddenly, the guests heard beautiful piano music coming from the second floor. "One of the men went upstairs to find the source of the music. By the time he reached the top of the stairs, the music had stopped. At first, he thought it was coming from the antique piano in the hallway, but no one was upstairs, and there were no electric cords leading from the piano to an outlet in the wall." One of the guests asked McShane if she could have a copy of the CD playing upstairs. With a confused look on her face, McShane said, "There is no CD player upstairs."

*Guests heard spectral music coming from this piano during a party.* (Courtesy Marilyn Brown)

One of the most haunted rooms in the house is a bedroom on the second floor. One morning, a docent pulled up the drive, and she saw a lady standing in an upstairs window. The docent thought it was the tour guide she was supposed to be working with that day, so she waved to her and walked inside. She called out, "I'm here." When she got no reply, she went upstairs to see if her partner was O.K. No one was there, so she returned downstairs and looked out a window. There was her partner, walking up the driveway. The docent opened the door and said, "I could have sworn I saw you standing in the window." Her partner replied, "It wasn't me."

In 2007, a group of paranormal investigators came to the Richards DAR House to conduct an investigation. They brought with them a reporter from the *Mobile Bay Monthly*. The group began their investigation in the upstairs bedroom where the ghostly woman had appeared in the window. "The group began by asking the question,

'If someone is here, give us a sign,'" McShane said. "A thunderstorm was building up. Every time they asked the question, there was a crash of thunder, and lightning flashed across the sky. One of the ladies on the team said, 'Let's move on. We'll come back to this room later.' So they picked up their gear and moved to another room. The guy from *Mobile Bay Monthly* set up a camera in the doorway. He set the timer so that the camera would go off every few seconds. He turned around to walk off, and lightning lit up the room again. He looked at the photos on the camera, and he saw a big glowing oval-shaped object in one of the pictures. He thought it could have been a reflection in the mirror, but he wasn't sure. The reporter called his editor, and she said, 'Let's put it on the computer and blow it up.' In the blowup, you can see a man with a long coat looking out the window." The group showed the photo to several other paranormal investigators, who theorized that one of the spirits in the house used the energy generated by the lightning to appear. A number of other paranormal groups have tried unsuccessfully to recreate the photograph.

One or two years after the photograph was published, McShane was standing in the doorway of the middle bedroom on the second floor when her sister began teasing her about being in the "ghost room." "I finally got fed up with her picking on me," McShane said. "I turned to her—she was standing in the doorway—and I said, 'You know I don't believe in ghosts!' As soon as I got that out of my mouth, we heard a loud 'boom!' I turned around. There was a little book on that dresser, and that book had somehow fallen off and landed several feet away in the middle of the floor. One of the trains that come down to the dock could have shaken the dresser, I suppose. I could see the book falling off the dresser but not jumping all the way to the middle of the floor. So that freaked me out. My sister's eyes were so big! I said, 'I know what just happened, and all I'm going to say, Captain Richards, is that I'm sorry and I will never again say, "I don't believe."'"

Captain Richards is not the only spirit that walks the halls of the Richards DAR House. A small bedroom called the "Boys' Room" is haunted by the ghosts of children who possibly died in the home. McShane told the story of a paranormal group who placed some marbles on the bed and began asking the children to move them. After a couple of minutes, nothing happened, so they put the red marble in the middle of the bed and promised to leave if the marble moved. "They waited a few minutes and, sure enough, the marble moved," McShane said. "They left the house and returned a couple of hours later. The red marble was gone, and we have never found it."

Nothing bad has ever happened to McShane in the Richards DAR House. However, her experience with the book falling off the dresser taught her to show more respect for the home's resident spirits. "I think the ghosts were trying to send me a message," she said, "and that message was, 'Be careful what you say.'"

## Spence-Moon House
## Livingston

The Spence-Moon House was built in 1834 on eighty acres of land for James H. Spence. Artisans from Connecticut and New Hampshire built this house and ten others on land that became available for settlement following the signing of the Treaty of Dancing Rabbit Creek in 1830. The daughter of the next owner of the home, William W. Hill, moved in with her husband, Samuel Inge, in 1852. He was a politician who served in the state legislature in 1844 and the United States Congress in 1847. Another notable occupant of the house was W. A. C. Jones, an engineer who built the Alamuchee-Bellamy Covered Bridge that is now on the campus of the University of West Alabama. He lived here from 1888 until 1905. Martha Fluker, who was one of the last owners of the house, had fond memories of it in the early twentieth century. "Once father planted princess feathers in front of the house that grew to be at least eight feet tall. My sister and I pretended that we lived in a medieval forest."

The Sumter County Historical Society now owns the Spence-Moon

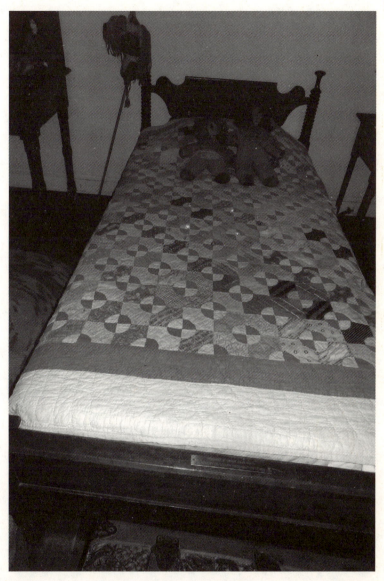

*A red marble placed on this bed in the "Boys' Room" of the Richards DAR House disappeared. It was never found.* (Courtesy Marilyn Brown)

House. Today, it is used for special events by the community and the University of West Alabama. It is important from an architectural viewpoint because it is one of only five Federal-period homes still standing in the area. These elements include the applique of urns, garlands, and rosettes on mantelpieces, doors, and windows. The kitchen was moved inside the house in the late nineteenth century.

The home is maintained by university students who live in it and keep it clean. One of these caretakers said that in 2011, he got up in the middle of the night to go to the restroom. While he was standing at the toilet, he felt someone breathing down his neck. He whipped his head around, but no one was there.

That same year, another young caretaker had a strange experience when he was spending the weekend alone in the house. Friday night, he was awakened by a loud noise coming from his friend's bedroom. When he opened the door, he was surprised to find the television on. What was even more strange was the fact that it was tuned to the Home Shopping Network. The young man's friend only watched

*The caretakers at the Spence-Moon House have complained about a ghostly presence that enjoys changing the television channels.*

ESPN. The next morning, he called his friend and was told that he was watching ESPN when he turned off the television and left. One of the boys said that the disturbances ceased after Susie Moon's picture was moved to the north parlor.

## Spring Villa
## Opelika

Situated on the outskirts of Opelika, Spring Villa is one of the few remaining examples of Gothic Revival architecture in the state. The house was designed by Andrew Jackson Dowling. Horace King built the Carpenter Gothic plantation home beside a spring-fed lake for William Penn Yonge in 1850. King was a part African/part Catawba Indian slave who was once owned by John Godwin. Gables crowned with a diamond-shaped pinnacle were placed on each of the four sides of the one-and-a-half-story wood-frame building. Additional distinctive features include stuccoed chimneys, three bays, and saw-work balconies fronting each window. In 1927, Spring Villa was acquired by the city of Opelika. In an effort to convert Spring Villa into a clubhouse in 1934, the Civil Works Administration added a four-bay façade on the centrally placed rear ell. Today, Spring Villa is the centerpiece of a 350-acre park at 1474 Lee Road 148, although the lake next to the house has dried up due to quarry mining a few miles away.

The ghost of Penn Yonge is still an active presence at Spring Villa. He had the reputation of being a cruel slave master who seemed to delight in punishing wayward slaves. One day in 1864, one of his slaves exacted revenge on the man who had made his life and those of his loved ones so miserable. He waited until Yonge's family was visiting relatives to put his plan into motion. "On this day, Yonge was all alone in the house," said Jeff Pokorney, who has served as caretaker of Spring Villa since 1997. "He had put in a long day of work, and he was tired. When it got dark, he started climbing the stairs to his bedroom upstairs. When he reached the thirteenth step, his slave stabbed him to death. When you walk up the stairs, you can

*Spring Villa was built in the Carpenter Gothic style for William Penn Yonge.* (Photo from en.wikipedia.org)

see the cubbyhole where the slave hid." After committing the crime, the slave ran off. Fearing retribution from their master's family, the other slaves captured him and hanged him. In the book *Haunted Auburn and Opelika*, authors Faith Serafin, Michelle Smith, and John Mark Poe write that the vengeful slave can still be seen wandering around the plantation, looking for an avenue of escape.

Barbara Kent, program director of Opelika's Parks and Recreation Department, said, "There are a lot of people around here who'll swear Spring Villa's haunted and that they've seen the ghosts. I don't really know what it is, but there's definitely something going on in that house." Yonge's ghost is the most commonly sighted spirit at Spring Villa. Most of the eyewitnesses describe the apparition as a tall, older man wearing a black coat and a top hat. He is usually seen strolling across the grounds of his former estate. Pokorney stated to me that his wife and sister-in-law saw an elderly man standing on the front porch. "They told me about him, and I ran out of the house, but I didn't see anybody there," Pokorney said. "There's no way anyone could have gotten away that fast. Whoever it was must've just disappeared." Not surprisingly, the thirteenth step on the staircase where Yonge was murdered is also supposed to be haunted. People say that the spectral footsteps always stop at that step.

Appropriately, Yonge's ghost was also sighted during a bad storm that knocked out the electricity inside the house. At the time, a number of young campers were staying there. The Parks and Recreation crew and counselors decided that the best course was to remain inside until the storm blew over. When the weather cleared, the children were led outside. A young counselor nicknamed "Mystic Mike" decided to run back inside to make sure that everything was secure. A few minutes later, he walked onto the porch. Bill Harrelson, director of Opelika's Parks and Recreation Department, said, "He was white as a sheet and looked like he was going to faint." Once Mike regained his composure, he said that when he entered the children's sleeping quarters, he saw a spectral figure playing a piano. Within a few seconds, both the piano player and the piano vanished. Harrelson said, "You talk about someone being scared. The hairs on the back of his neck were standing straight up. He was so scared that he could hardly talk. He never went back into that house again."

Because of recent break-ins by vandals and burglars, Spring Villa is locked up most of the time. Pokorney opens the doors once in a while for ghost hunters bent on conducting all-night investigations inside the old mansion. He recalled one particular group that used a flashlight to communicate with the spirits. "The investigators said, 'If you're here, turn the flashlight on,' and the flashlight came on." Pokorney is not particularly concerned if investigators make contact with the plantation's ghosts. "If they want to find a ghost," he said, "that is fine with me."

## Sturdivant Hall
## Selma

Sturdivant Hall was built between 1852 and 1856 for Col. Edward

T. Watts. The Greek Revival mansion was designed by architect Thomas Helm Lee, a Selma resident and cousin of Robert E. Lee. The plaster and iron work was done by Italian artists and craftsmen. Colonel Watts lived in the house until 1864, when he moved his family to Texas. The mansion was purchased by John McGee Parkman, who paid $465,000 for it on February 12, 1864. He was president of the First National Bank of Selma when Reconstruction came to Alabama. In 1867, Parkman was accused by the military governor of Alabama, Wager Swayne, of embezzling Federal funds that had been deposited in the bank. According to Alabama folklorist Kathryn Tucker Windham, author of *13 Alabama Ghosts and Jeffrey* (1969), Parkman was imprisoned in Castle Morgan in Cahaba. Several of Parkman's friends, who believed that he should not have been incarcerated for making bad business decisions, concocted an elaborate scheme to free him. On May 23, 1867, they held an impromptu parade in front of the jail to distract the jailers. While the guards were watching the jugglers and singers, Parkman sneaked out. After a few minutes, the jailers pursued Parkman to the riverbank near the Cahaba wharf, where a steamboat was waiting for him. The circumstances of Parkman's death are unclear. Some say that he was shot as he dove into the Cahaba River. Others say that soon after entered the water, he was crushed by the paddle of the steamboat. Some believe that Parkman's friends killed him to prevent him from revealing their involvement in the botched escape. Only a few residents of Selma believe that Parkman made his way to freedom.

The mansion changed hands in January 1870 when a Selma merchant named Emile Gillman purchased it for $12,000. The house remained in the Gillman family until 1957, when the city of Selma bought it for $75,000. The purchase was made with the help of a $50,000 bequest from the estate of Robert Daniel Sturdivant, who wanted the family home to be converted into a house museum. Today, the city of Selma has the responsibility of maintaining the antebellum home.

The ten-room, 6,000-square-foot mansion is now run as a house museum. The docents of Sturdivant Hall say that it is haunted by a number of ghosts. The full-body apparition of John McGee Parkman has been seen inside the house, mostly upstairs. He occasionally appears in his daughters' bedroom. Visitors have sighted him up in the cupola, too. He has never been seen outside of the house. Longtime docent Pat Tate told me that most of the poltergeist-like activity in the mansion is blamed on Parkman's ghost. Most of the time, she and other staff members heard him walking around upstairs. They also heard doors open and close on their own. On one occasion, the doors opened when a crowd of people was in the mansion. One night, a maid made the bed in one of rooms before she went home. The next morning, she was shocked to find the imprint of a body on the bed. Several people have seen flashes of light inside the house. When strange things happened, the staff would say, "Good evening, Mr. Parkman." The activity usually stopped.

The ghost of John McGee Parkman may also be responsible for one of the most terrifying incidents that have occurred inside the house. One day, the Orkin man was spraying upstairs while the docents were downstairs. After a few minutes, he ran down the stairs. He said somebody pushed him, and he refused to go back up. He exited the mansion in such a hurry that he left all of his equipment behind.

One legend that seems to defy attempts to debunk it is the story of Parkman's burial. "We have heard stories that he was buried in the scuppernong orchard in the back, but that's not true," Tate said. "There's also a story that they never found Parkman's body. That's not true either. He is buried in Live Oak Cemetery." For years, though, many people have insisted that Parkman is actually buried behind the house. An elderly man named Adolf, who worked at Sturdivant Hall in the 1950s, said that one time, his grandfather plowed in the back garden after the Parkmans left. "Adolf's grandfather said that the mule would come to a [certain] place and would rare up and would not go forward," Tate said. "And that was where Mr. Parkman had been buried. He was convinced that he was there. And when he worked here, he would never, never go out in that garden."

The ghosts of the Parkmans' children also make frequent appearances inside Sturdivant Hall. They are often sighted staring out of a window on the second floor. Tate told the story about such a sighting that occurred during a "Battle Ball" for a reenactment of the Battle of Selma. "They always had guards posted in the study so that children would not go upstairs, which were off-limits. Well, I noticed that one of the guards was missing, so when he came back, I questioned him, and he said that he had three people tell him that they had seen children upstairs looking out the window. And he had gone up to check, and there were no children."

Tate also told the story of a sighting of the children that occurred in the late 1950s. "One of the commanders out at Maxwell Air Force Base came out here to meet somebody. They looked up, and they saw children standing in a widow of an upstairs room. They said they heard noises too. When they came in with their key, they went upstairs, and there was no one there."

A ghost has been encountered in Sturdivant Hall much more recently. "Several months ago, we had a group of young people

*People have seen the ghostly figures of John McGee Parkman's young daughters staring out of the windows of Sturdivant Hall.* (Photo from Wikimedia Commons)

standing in the hall," Tate said. "And we had a tremendous painting sitting on an easel. Nobody was standing near it, and it just jumped off and broke into a hundred pieces. The children could not be convinced that it was not Mr. Parkman who had knocked it off."

## Sweetwater Mansion
## Florence

The land on which Sweetwater Mansion stands was called "Sweetwater" by the local Indians. Construction of the house was begun in 1828 by John Brahan, who had served as a major general in the War of 1812. At the time of his death, only the first floor up to the windowsills of what was to become a two-story, eight-room house was completed. His son, Maj. Robert Brahan, inherited the property. However, Major Brahan chose not to live there, so he gave Sweetwater Mansion to his sister's husband, Robert Miller Patton. In 1835, Patton and his wife, Jane Locke Brahan Patton, completed the house. During the Civil War, both the Confederate and Union armies occupied Sweetwater Mansion. On November 3, 1863, one of Gen. William Tecumseh Sherman's divisions camped there. The soldiers helped themselves to everything they could carry, including Mrs. Patton's purse containing forty dollars, jewels, and three diamond studs belonging to her son, Billy, who was killed during the Battle of Shiloh.

In 1864, Gen. John Bell Hood established his headquarters at Florence. That year, during a military ball, Confederate general Gideon Pillow made an indelible contribution to the lore of Sweetwater Mansion when he tripped and fell over the iron railing into the basin of a fountain in the center of the front walk. By the time the war ended, the basement had been used as a hospital. It also served as Lauderdale County's first jail.

After the Civil War, Robert M. Patton became governor of Alabama. The Pattons lived in Sweetwater Mansion for many years before passing the house down to their daughter, Martha Hayes

Patton, and her husband, Col. John David Weeden. After their death, their son, John Dowling Weeden, and his wife, Jessie Ora Earthman Weeden, became the next owners of the home. John Weeden lived there until he died in 1960. The Patton-Weeden family's 137-year ownership of Sweetwater Mansion came to an end with Jessie Weeden's death in 1972. The Weedens' daughter, Elizabeth, chose not to live in the historic home.

Emmer Lettie Region served as caretaker of Sweetwater Mansion until her death at age seventy-four in 2004. People said that she protected the house with a pistol that she kept in her apron pocket. She was a key player in the mansion's best-known ghost story. Legend has it that one evening, she had just entered the parlor when she had a vision of a young man lying in a casket. She could clearly see where a bullet had entered his head. Later, Lettie found out that the wake for Robert and Jane Patton's son, Billy, had been held in the parlor. His coffin had been placed in the same spot where Lettie saw it. When it dawned on her that she had had a brush with the paranormal, Lettie never ventured from the two rooms where she lived. According to one legend, she even went so far as to nail one of her doors shut to keep the house's spirits out of her rooms. Friends of Lettie offer a different explanation for her decision to reside in only two rooms. They say that she stayed there because the rooms had an air conditioner and a heater.

Over the years, other ghost stories have surfaced as well. Apparently the face of a woman christened "the porcelain lady" has slowly appeared on the wallpaper. One night, several employees smelled something burning in the house. They traced the foul odor to the kitchen, which had caught on fire in the 1970s. One of the employees took a photograph of the kitchen and was shocked to see flames in the images. Visitors and employees have also reported sightings of shadow figures and the full-body apparition of a woman wearing a nineteenth-century dress. People have also heard spectral whispers and the laughing of children. Objects left overnight in one location have turned up in an entirely different spot the next morning. Doors have slammed on their own when no one was near. One witness saw

*The face of a woman known as the "porcelain lady" gradually appeared on the wallpaper of Sweetwater Mansion.* (Photo from fingerparanormal.wordpress.org)

the ghostly figure of a Civil War soldier sitting on a log. He was holding a cannon's ramrod in his right hand.

Cynthia Johnson, the current director of Sweetwater Mansion, has allowed a number of paranormal groups to investigate the hauntings. Some of these individuals have captured compelling evidence during their overnight stay. Robert Simone, who leads Ghost Hunters of the Southern Territories (G.H.O.S.T.) with his wife, Karen, claims to have been pushed down the steps by an invisible hand. On a different investigation, something threw a piece of the ceiling at him. He aimed his camera in the direction the pieces had come from and snapped the shutter. The camera captured the image of two small children. His most bizarre encounter occurred one night when he was sitting in the main parlor. Two chairs were sitting in front of him. Two cameras that take photographs every three seconds were placed in the parlor. Two of the photographs taken three seconds apart showed one of the chairs in one spot and then in an entirely different spot. In one of the EVP's recorded by Robert and Karen, the voice of someone saying "Silverman" is very clear. Records showed that a man named Solverman had signed a deed to the house in 1914.

The ghosts of Sweetwater Mansion received national attention in 2012 with the broadcast of an investigation of the historic house on the television program *Paranormal State*. The investigators heard the eerie sound of a board sliding across the floor, the sound of a person falling on the floor, and spectral footsteps. They also saw a door move on its own. All of the investigators were overcome by what can best be described as a "heavy feeling" on the second floor. The years of testimonies and evidence suggest that the tragic past of Sweetwater Mansion is still resonating in the present.

## The Weeden House
### Huntsville

One of Huntsville's most historically significant homes is the Weeden House. It was built in 1819 in the Federalist style for Huntsville entrepreneur Henry C. Bradford. He was forced to sell the house to John Read in 1820 following the loss of his mercantile business in the Panic of 1819. In 1824, the home was purchased by John McKinley, who went on to become an associate justice of the U.S. Supreme Court. Three years later, the president of the Huntsville Bank, Bartley M. Lowe, moved into the house. His portrait by John Grimes is prominently displayed there. The next owner, Martha Chambers Betts, sold the home to Dr. William Weeden in 1845. At the time he purchased the house, the property stretched from Gates Street to Weeden Street. His wife, Jane Eliza Brooks Urquhart, transformed the yard into one of the city's most beautiful gardens. The house remained in the Weeden family until 1956, when it was purchased at public auction by Mrs. B. A. Stockton. She sold the house to the Twickenham Historic Preservation District Association in 1973. The Huntsville Housing Authority took over the old home in 1976. The Weeden House has been open to the public since 1981. Some docents and visitors believe that the home is still inhabited by the ghost of its most famous occupant.

Maria Howard Weeden was born in 1846, six months after Dr. Weeden's death. She was educated at Huntsville Female Academy, where she exhibited a talent for painting. Eager to develop Maria's gift, Mrs. Weeden hired a local portraitist, William Frye, to give her private lessons.

During the Federal occupation of Huntsville in 1862, Maria and her family moved to her older sister's Tuskegee plantation. When they returned to their Huntsville home in 1866, Maria helped support the family by giving art lessons and painting notecards. She also painted 200 species of wildflowers growing on nearby Monte Sano. She submitted inspirational poems to the *Christian Observer*. Outraged by the way artists were depicting freedmen and women as caricatures at the World's Columbian Exposition in Chicago, she

*Passersby have seen ghostly faces staring out of the windows of the house once occupied by artist Maria Howard Weeden.* (Courtesy Wikimedia Commons)

began painting realistic portraits of the type of freed people she had known all of her life. In 1897, her art was published in a book titled *Shadows on the Wall*. Other published collections of her paintings followed, including *Bandanna Ballads* (1899), *Songs of the Old South* (1901), and *Old Voices* (1904). Maria died in the Weeden House, in the room where she had lived most of her life, on April 12, 1905. She was buried in Maple Hill Cemetery in Huntsville.

Even in Maria Howard Weeden's lifetime, the old house had a reputation for being "strange." It was known as a "weeping house" because paint will not adhere to certain parts of its exterior. Ghostly activity occurs inside as well. Lynn Williams, the director of the Weeden House Museum and Garden, said that a chair in one of the upper rooms has been known to change locations during the night. Two women who were taking a tour were listening to the docent relate the history of the house when they were frightened by the chiming of a grandfather clock that had not worked in years. Passersby have reported seeing spectral figures staring out of the windows. One of these apparitions appears to be a man wringing his hands. Docents who have stayed late have heard phantom footsteps inside the house. It is little wonder that Spirit House Tours of the Weeden House Museum and Garden were given October 30-November 1 in 2013.

# Chapter 2

# Haunted Colleges and Universities

## Athens State University
### Athens

In 1822, the Athens Female Academy was established on land donated by Alabama Supreme Court Judge John McKinley. The school that was to become Athens State University began as a four-room schoolhouse. The mission of the academy was to provide an education for the girls and young ladies of Alabama on the elementary, secondary, and collegiate levels. In 1842, the trustees of the Athens Female Academy planned to become affiliated with the Methodist Church in order to attract students from a broader geographical area. In 1843, the Alabama legislature ratified the name change to Athens Female Institute of the Tennessee Annual Conference. The institution's first president was Richard Henderson. The first building on campus, Founders Hall, was constructed with funds donated by local residents. The student body gradually increased from eighty to over two hundred students by the 1850s. Jane Hamilton Childs, the former head of the Huntsville Female College, became president of the Athens Female Institute in 1858. Under its new name—the Athens Collegiate Institute—the school kept its doors open through the Civil War. By the time Childs retired in 1869, the institute had once again adopted the policy of serving only those girls whose families could afford the tuition. In 1870, the North Alabama Conference of the Methodist Church assumed control of the school, renaming it the North Alabama Female College. The Alabama legislature changed the name to the Athens Female Institute in 1872 and to Athens Female College in 1889. Financial problems plagued the school through the turn of the century.

The college's fortunes began to improve in the twentieth century. Mary Norman Moore became president in 1904. Under her leadership, the school discontinued elementary education. It received accreditation from the Southern Association and Schools in 1911. That same year, concert pianist Kat McCandless was hired to build the music program. In 1913, the Methodist Conference raised the school to Class A status, which carried with it a minimum endowment of $100,000. The school was renamed Athens College for Women in 1915. Moore stepped down as president in 1916; she returned in 1925 following the death of her husband. She retired in 1930 as the only person to have served two terms as president.

Moore's replacement, Eugene R. Naylor, was the first male academic to be appointed president. In one of his first acts as president, he made the drastic move to increase enrollment by admitting male students. Therefore, the name was changed to Athens College in 1939. Naylor then set about improving the quality of the school's programs. After his retirement in 1949, succeeding presidents strove to continue upgrading the curriculum.

When Sidney E. Sandridge was appointed president in 1970, the school was experiencing a funding crisis. After the state of Alabama took control of the school in 1975, the legislature changed the name to Athens State College. In addition, the school became an upper-division two-year college within the state's community college system. Calhoun Community College president James Chastain replaced Sandridge as president in 1981. Nine years later, he was replaced by Jerry F. Bartlett, who brought distance-learning technology to the school. In 1998, the school was renamed Athens State University.

Today, students attending Athens State University can choose from over forty undergraduate majors. Intercollegiate sports were discontinued in the 2003-4 academic year, but other extracurricular activities are offered, such as more than thirty-five clubs. Students also entertain themselves by passing down the university's ghost stories.

Founders Hall is the oldest and most legendary of all the buildings on campus. Sandra Cook, who works in the President's Office, told me, "The whole community joined in to build Founders Hall in 1822 because they wanted a place where their girls could grow to be Southern belles." One of the best known of the building's legends concerns its columns. "The columns in the front of it are named Matthew, Mark, Luke, and John because at that time, it was a religious school and was under the auspices of the Methodist Church until 1975. One of the columns supposedly has a keg of whiskey in it. The story goes that the brick mason who was working there liked to have a little nip now and then. One day, the supervisor came by, so he tossed the keg of whiskey in the column, and it's still there." Like a number of other Southern heroines who are reputed to have stood up to the Yankees, Madame Jane Hamilton Childs, the headmistress, is said to have used her wits to save Founders Hall. The story goes that Gen. Ivan Turchaninov, who was a Russian on the side of the Yankee troops who occupied Athens, had come to burn and destroy Founders Hall. Madame Childs marched out on the lawn and from the folds of her long black skirt, she took a note, supposedly from Abraham Lincoln. After that, the soldiers left. "We've not found the note," Cook said. "It may be stuck away in the archives somewhere."

Founders Hall's most popular stories these days are its ghost stories. Most of the sightings in the building center around a young woman who sneaked out of Founders Hall after the Civil War with her girlfriends to meet their boyfriends. As the girls were making their way down the staircase in the dim light generated by the candles they were holding, a sudden gust of wind ignited the long hair of one of the students. She screamed and tumbled down the stairs. She died a short while later. The ghost of the unfortunate young lady is credited with most of the paranormal activity inside Founders Hall. Students have heard phantom footsteps, clicking sounds, and squeaking doors. Cold spots have popped up throughout the building. Lights turn off and on by themselves. Students have also felt puffs of cold air and smelled smoke. The apparition of a female figure has been seen standing at the building's windows. Sandra Cook said that according to two professors, working after hours inside Founders Hall is risky. "One professor was here late one night when he heard the jingling of keys outside his office. When he opened the door, he saw something like a fog standing there. Another professor who came to the college to find a job was staying here overnight when he heard footsteps and the rustling of chains. He left the premises and never came back."

Brown Hall is a much smaller building than Founders Hall, but it is also associated with a courageous woman's heroic stand. Built in 1912, Brown Hall is named after Florence Brown, who was secretary to the president in the early 1900s. In 1909, the school was beset by a typhoid epidemic. It closed, and all of the students left except for four young ladies who were unable to return home. Knowing that the girls required medical attention, Florence stayed behind and tended to their needs. All four young women—and Florence Brown—died in the epidemic.

Today, Brown Hall is used for administrative offices. In the past it was used for continuing-education classes. "One of the persons who

*The ghost of a female student who fell down the stairs late at night and died is said to be responsible for most of the paranormal activity in Founders Hall.* (Photo from Wikimedia Commons)

taught art classes in that building told us after we moved in, 'Don't ever stay too late because strange things happen here,'" Cook said. "Then he gave us some of the details. For example, he said if he had a night class and laid something down—he knew exactly where it was—the next day it might be moved or in another room. On one occasion, it was kind of a chain reaction. He was in the room late at night, and something started happening. It just sort of went around the entire room. Pictures fell, someone knocked on a trashcan—sort of a domino effect, I guess." Other paranormal events range from portraits taking on an evil appearance to microwaves and computers unplugging themselves.

Athens State University's most famous ghost is the spirit of a young opera singer named Abigail Burns. The story goes that she performed in the auditorium at McCandless Hall shortly after the building was dedicated in 1914. After her performance, which was greeted by enthusiastic applause, Abigail was holding a bouquet of roses when she vowed to return some day. As dark clouds rolled in, Abigail climbed into her carriage and rode out of town. As her carriage crossed a bridge over a gorge, lightning flashed across the sky, causing the horse to bolt. The carriage careened off the bridge to the rocks below, killing Abigail and her driver. Generations of students claim to have seen the apparition of Abigail Burns standing in one of the third-floor windows of McCandless Hall. She is usually described as a blonde woman wearing a long, white gown and holding a bouquet of roses. Sometimes, her ghost is bathed in an eerie light. Some students even claim to have smelled the flowers. In 1997, Mark Dunn, a professor at Athens State University, researched the legend. He discovered that an operatic performance was held at McCandless Hall in 1914, but he could not find any of Abigail Burns' death records. The absence of historical fact has not discouraged students from telling the story of Abigail. "The stories are not told as much now as they were in the sixties and seventies," Cook said, "but they are told in dormitories in close-knit groups. We have had people come from Birmingham during Halloween to catch a glimpse of her."

In 2013, local television station WAFF Channel 48 teamed up

*The ghost of opera singer Abigail Burns has been seen standing in one of the windows of McCandless Hall, holding a bouquet of roses.* (Photo from Wikimedia Commons)

with Syfy's *Deep South Paranormal* to investigate the reports of ghostly activity at Athens State University. At Brown Hall, the investigators tried to communicate with the resident ghosts by using a spirit box, which allows spirits to speak through the white noise. When one member of the group, Jon Hodges, asked the name of the city the investigators were in, the box said, "Athens." The investigators then moved to Founders Hall. On the third floor, group member Keith Ramsey asked any resident ghost for permission to play music. A WAFF camera captured a voice saying, "O.K." The paranormal activity escalated when the investigators placed a flashlight on the floor in different parts of the third floor and began asking questions. The flashlight turned on three times in a span of ten minutes. The next day, WAFF reporter Nick Lough could not say for certain that the buildings he stayed in were haunted, but he admitted to having had several personal experiences that he could not explain away.

## Auburn University
## Auburn

The Alabama legislature founded Auburn University on February 1, 1856. East Alabama Male College, as it was originally called, was operated by the Methodist Church. Rev. William J. Sasnett served as the school's first president.

The school opened in the fall of 1859 with eighty students and ten faculty members. It closed during the Civil War because most of the students enlisted. "Old Main," the first building on Auburn's campus, was transformed from a dormitory into a field hospital. The campus itself was used as a training ground for the Confederate Army. Six years after the school reopened in 1866, the state of Alabama took it over. That same year, the school was declared a land-grant institution under the provisions of the Morrill Act. As a result, the name was changed to the Agricultural and Mechanical College of Alabama. Throughout the remainder of the nineteenth century, most of the students were enrolled in the cadet program. In 1887, Old Main burned and was replaced by Samford Hall. In 1892, football became a varsity sport, and women were admitted to the school. In 1899, the name was changed to Alabama Polytechnic Institute. During World War I, 878 males attended the school as soldier students. Enlisted men received training in mechanics and radio there. Like most institutions of higher learning, the school experienced serious financial problems in the Great Depression. During this time, Pres. Bradford Knapp's ambitious building program was put on hold, and faculty salaries were cut. World War II brought sweeping changes to the university. To meet the need for engineers and scientists, the school added the Engineering, Science, and Management War Training (ESMWT) program to the curriculum. Between 1945 and 1950, thousands of veterans enrolled in the college on the GI Bill. Because the university was offering courses in fields other than agriculture and mechanics, its name was changed to Auburn University by the Alabama legislature in 1960. Segregation came to an end at the university in 1964 when the first

African-American students were admitted. By the 2010s, the student body had expanded to over 23,000 students; the faculty included more than 1,200 instructors and professors.

The setting of Auburn's signature ghost story is the University Chapel. Built in 1851 as a Presbyterian church, the chapel is the oldest building on campus. In 1864, Sydney Grimlett was brought to the Presbyterian church for the treatment of a leg wound he suffered while fighting with the Sixth Virginia Cavalry during the Atlanta Campaign. Because Dr. L. A. Bryan had more than three hundred patients to treat, he was unable to get to Sydney right away. As a result, gangrene set in, and Sydney's leg had to be amputated. He died a few hours later inside the church. Over the next sixty years, the church was used for classroom space and even as a YMCA. Then in 1926, a theatrical group named the Auburn Players moved in, and they continued to use the building for the next forty-seven years. Some people say that Sydney was inadvertently lured back to the church after the production of a nineteenth-century English play. Sydney continued to make his presence known in the 1960s and 1970s by whistling in the attic, moving scenery, stamping with his one remaining foot, and causing props to malfunction. On one memorable evening, an eerie green light hovered near the ceiling during a production of Eugene O'Neill's play *Long Day's Journey into Night*. The identity of the theater's resident ghost was unknown until a group of young actors consulted a Ouija board and it spelled out Sydney's name. His presence was so much a part of the Auburn Players that the award for the most outstanding drama student was named "The Sydney Award." Whoever the spirit was, he evidently left the premises after the building was rededicated as the University Chapel.

## Bevill State Community College
### Jasper

Dr. Carl Jesse founded Walker College in 1938. Davis Hall, built in 1941, served as the classroom building for many years. The funds for its construction were provided by a grant from the Federal

Works Progress Administration. During the building's first year of existence, four faculty members and forty-five students attended classes in Davis Hall. Following Dr. Jesse's death in 1955, the college's second president, Dr. David Rowland, nurtured the growth of the college through his innovative fundraising efforts, such as a two-dollar-bill campaign and a silver-dollar campaign. In December 1993, the University of Alabama initiated plans to acquire Walker College. Bevill State Community College absorbed Walker College in 1998.

The paranormal activity reported in Davis Hall could possibly be traced back to 1955, when Dr. Carl Jesse's body lay in state on the second floor. For many years, the stately old building remained empty until the college received federal grant money to renovate it to house the Department of Broadcasting and Journalism. During the renovations in the early 1990s, students began reporting strange occurrences in the building, such as papers flying off a music stand when the vent was closed and brand-new pieces of equipment turning on and off by themselves. Moving shadows were seen in rooms where all the windows were blacked out due to the studio lighting.

Pamela Decker was a student here in the early 1990s. Late one evening, she and a friend were in Davis Hall when they heard phantom footsteps echoing in the hallways behind them. Elevators would run by themselves, and when the doors opened, no one was there. Pamela said she felt a presence on the stairs, as if someone was walking behind her. One of the scariest places in the building was the basement. "One day, I was standing at the vending machines in the basement when I saw someone walk by," Pamela told me. "I thought it was a maintenance worker or a janitor. I began talking to the person, but I was met with silence. I walked back to the area where I saw the person walking around. All the doors were locked, and no one else was in the basement." Over time, more and more students began hearing strange noises inside and outside of Davis Hall. A story about its haunting appeared in the 1993 Walker College yearbook, *Stars and Bars*.

After enough people began reporting unexplainable experiences inside Davis Hall, the stigma attached to having a paranormal encounter began to wear off. "When all these strange things began happening, we were pretty passive about them," Decker said. "We didn't discuss them for a long time. No one wanted to face the almost certain ridicule. But when we finally did have a group discussion, it turned out that almost everyone who were in the building had experienced something strange. Once the topic of a possible ghost came up, there was a feeling of release, a catharsis, I suppose."

## Huntingdon College
## Montgomery

On February 2, 1854, Gov. John Winston and the Alabama legislature established Tuskegee Female College in Tuskegee, Alabama. Andrew Adgate Lipscomb, the first president, shaped the college into a teaching institution. In 1856, the first graduating class consisted of 4 students. Three years later, the enrollment rose to 216 students. When the United Methodist Church took control of the college in 1872, the school's name was changed to Alabama Conference Female College. By the turn of the century, the college had outgrown its Tuskegee campus. In 1906, the president, Dr. John Massey, initiated the search for a better location. Two years later, Dr. John Sellers, William Moore, and C. G. Zirkle purchased fifty acres of land in the Cloverdale neighborhood of Montgomery from J. G. Thomas and donated the parcel to the college.

Frederick Law Olmsted, Jr., was hired in 1908 to design the campus. On August 24, the administration relocated equipment, furniture, and college records to a rented building that was chosen as the temporary home of the college. Following a devastating fire that destroyed the building and all of its contents in 1909, Pres. William Martin and the entire student body moved to Sullins College in Virginia. In 1910, the first building at the Montgomery campus, John Jefferson Flowers Memorial Hall, was completed, and the college opened its doors under a new name, the Women's College of Alabama. The architect, H. Langsford Warren, designed the building in the same Gothic style used at Cambridge and Oxford universities in England. The college remained an all-female institution until 1934, when it graduated its first male student. However, the first full-time students were not admitted until 1954. To reflect the college's coed population, the board decided in 1935 to change the name to Huntingdon College, in honor of Selina, countess of Huntingdon, who was instrumental in spreading Methodism in England. A number of buildings have been constructed at Huntingdon College since the 1940s, including Julia Walker Russell Dining Hall (1963), Hubert F. Searcy Hall (1970), James W. Wilson Center (1987), and Carolyn and Wynton Blount Hall (1995). To accommodate its rapid growth, the college acquired the thirteen-acre Cloverdale School property. Today, Huntingdon College has more than twenty undergraduate programs. The college has built on its strengths, especially its liberal arts, pre-law and pre-medical sciences programs. Huntingdon College is also noteworthy for Gothic Revival and Tudor Revival buildings, one of which—Pratt Hall—holds a prominent place in the state's ghost lore because of the Red Lady.

The Red Lady is, without a doubt, Alabama's best-known college ghost. This particular story began at the college's Tuskegee campus in the nineteenth century. The first sighting took place at 10:00 P.M. on "Sky Alley," the top floor of the Tuskegee dormitory. Several young women stared in horror as the female specter, wearing a red dress and holding a red parasol, strolled down the hall. The red glow emanating from her crimson figure illuminated the dark hallway. The silent spirit seemed to be oblivious to the girls who were watching her. When the Red Lady reached the end of the hall and turned around, the students ducked into an open dorm room and shut the door. Shaking uncontrollably, the girls huddled behind the door and listened to the clicking of the apparition's shoes as she walked up and down the hallway. After a few minutes, the footsteps faded away. The girls ran over to the window just in time to see the

Red Lady walk through a row of cedars and pass through the main gate.

According to Kathryn Tucker Windham's version of the tale in her book *13 Alabama Ghosts and Jeffrey*, the Red Lady was a wealthy young woman from New York. The story takes place in Pratt Hall, built in 1912 on the Montgomery campus of Huntingdon College. In the variants of the tale, she is known as either Martha or Margaret. She was forced to attend Huntingdon College by her father, who told her that she would not inherit his fortune unless she graduated from his mother's alma mater. She arrived at her dormitory, Pratt Hall, wearing a red dress. She brought with her red draperies. Her dorm mates were fascinated and somewhat put off by her room's red décor. Over the next few weeks, Martha seemed to go out of her way to isolate herself from her classmates. She ate by herself in the cafeteria and refused to interact with her roommate's friends when they visited in her room. Some say that Martha's apparent disdain for the other girls was actually shyness. Her roommate eventually tired of Martha's silent treatment and moved out. A succession of roommates moved in—and out—of Martha's room. They could not tolerate the girl's cold demeanor. The president of Pratt Hall took pity on Martha and moved in with her in an attempt to help her fit in with the rest of the residents. After a few weeks, she too found it impossible to live with the New York girl who seemed to be too good for Alabama. On her last day as Martha's roommate, she was packing her suitcase when Martha opened the door to enter. For a few seconds, Martha stood in the doorway, frozen to the spot. Finally, she pointed her finger at her roommate and said, "So, you are going to abandon me, just like the rest. Go ahead. Leave. I promise you that you will never forget this day for as long as you live."

Over the next few days, Martha began acting even more strangely than usual. Sometimes, she walked into the various dormitories late at night, opening the doors and staring in the darkness for a few minutes before moving on to the next room. One day, Martha failed to show up for classes or for meals in the cafeteria. Sensing that something was seriously wrong, her last roommate walked up to the fourth floor of Pratt Hall. She was passing down the gloomy hallway when suddenly, crimson flashes of light emanating from Martha's room punctuated the darkness. The girl cautiously made her way to her former room. When she opened the door, she was shocked to see Martha dressed in her red nightgown, sprawled on her bed. Dried blood encrusted the gashes on her wrists. Martha was dead, an apparent suicide. For decades, students living on the fourth floor of Pratt Hall claimed to have seen her spirit prowling the hallways, sometimes passing through walls or closed doors. Students also reported seeing red flashes of light coming from the transom of Martha's former room. All of these sightings occurred on the anniversary of Martha's suicide. A woman interviewed by this writer said that her daughter saw the red light back in the late 1970s when she stayed on the fourth floor during summer band camp.

Pratt Hall now houses the Department of Education and Psychology. Ironically, the offices of campus sororities are on the fourth floor, the same floor where the troubled girl from New York found it impossible to bond with the other residents. Even though Martha's former residence is no longer a dormitory, her tragic story lives on. Every October, the members of Phi Mu, Chi Omega, and Alpha Omicron Pi sororities hold a Red Lady Run. To commemorate the death of Huntingdon College's most legendary undergraduate, the sisters paint their faces, don black clothing, and run around the campus. Martha's memory also lives on in the stories that students and alumni tell each other on dark, stormy nights.

Martha may be the best known of Huntingdon College's ghosts, but she is not the only one. In recent years, the Houghton Library's mischievous spirit has begun receiving attention. Unlike Martha's, the library ghost's background is unknown. Its deep-throated moans have led students to believe that it is male. The ghost did not even have a name until the 1990s, when students began calling him "Frank." He is believed to be responsible for the poltergeist-like activity in the library, such as leaving opened books on the tables, slamming the heavy oak doors, pushing books off the shelves, moving objects from one place to another, and rolling an office chair around the library.

Frank may never achieve Martha's notoriety, but he is a very real presence to the people who work and study in the library.

## Spring Hill College
## Mobile

Spring Hill College is Mobile's oldest Catholic school and the first Catholic college in the Southeast. Michael Porter, Mobile's first bishop, founded the school in 1830 on a hill. He staffed it with two priests and four seminarians. He had originally envisioned the institution as a boarding school for boys under twelve years old. They would receive an education in mathematics, languages, geography, physics, chemistry, astronomy, and history. When he removed the age restriction, the campus population increased from 30 in 1830 to 130 in 1832. Jesuit priests from Lyon, France, took over teaching responsibilities in 1847. In 1932, Pres. Andrew Smith admitted nine African-American students to the college. Fannie Motley became its first African-American graduate. Notable alumni include chess champion and inventor Paul Morphy. Students are encouraged to engage in community service in the greater Mobile area. They also help others during their international service-immersion trips.

At least two parts of the college are haunted. The cemetery on campus contains the graves of priests who have taught here since the college was founded. According to one campus legend, the figure of a hooded monk has been seen hovering over the graves late at night. Spring Hill's best-known ghost story involves the spirit of a Jesuit priest, a Father Mueller, who taught in the mathematics department in Quinlan Hall. The longtime faculty member was one of the best-loved priests in the history of the school. After his death, his position was filled by a young priest who continued his predecessor's practice of giving extra credit to any student who could solve a seemingly unsolvable math problem. The next day, to the priest's surprise, a rather mediocre student named George slowly raised his hand. Concerned that the student would embarrass himself, the priest

*The ghost of a beloved mathematics teacher still makes appearances at Spring Hill College.* (Photo from Wikimedia Commons)

asked George if he was confident that he had the correct answer. George said he was and walked up to the blackboard. After George wrote on the board for a couple of minutes, the priest looked over his work and was surprised to see that George had solved the problem. When the priest asked the boy how he did it, George said that the night before, he was sitting in his dorm room, struggling with the problem, when an elderly priest walked in and showed him how to solve it. George then gave a perfect description of the priest who had just died. The old math professor's ghost has been seen many times since then, usually in the math department.

### Troy University
### Troy

The Alabama legislature established Troy State Normal School on February 26, 1887. Its first president was Joseph Macon Dill. It was renamed Troy State Normal College in 1893. The name was changed again, this time to Troy State Teachers College, in 1929, and it was moved to its present site. Enrollment more than doubled after World War II as a result of the influx of returning veterans whose education was funded by the GI Bill. To accommodate the new students, the college expanded its curriculum to include majors such as business. The word "Teachers" was removed from the college's name. Troy State College began offering extension courses on military bases in the 1950s. Several branch campuses were established over the next few years in Dothan, Phenix City, and Montgomery. The name was changed once again in 1967 to Troy State University after Gov. Lurleen Wallace removed the institution from control of the State Board of Education. The word "State" was removed from the name in 1982 to reflect the university's global mission. Today, Troy University is known for the high quality of its educational programs and for its haunted dormitories.

One of the university's oldest buildings is Shackelford Hall. Built in 1930, it was named after Edward M. Shackelford, who served as president from 1899 to 1936. The newly renovated suite dormitory is home to male and female students. The third floor of Shackelford is said to be haunted by a student named Sally Shack who hanged herself in the stairwell following her fiancé's death in one of the world wars. Sally's ghost is still an active presence in the lives of the residents, many of whom claim to have seen the melancholy spirit roaming the hallway on the third floor. Student Hunter Gregg told me about an incident that allegedly occurred in a room on the third floor of Shackelford Hall in the 1990s. "The two girls who were living there came back to their room after classes, and they saw two ink pens levitating off the table. They were so scared that they moved out of the room the next day."

Another haunted dormitory is Pace Hall. Named after Matthew Downer Pace, it was constructed in 1947 and renovated in 1998 as a Living and Learning Center for U.S. and international students. Pace Hall is known for its poltergeist activity. Sharrnique Mceachern, a broadcast journalism major from Ashville, said that one day in the early 1990s, two members of Phi Mu sorority, which was housed in the dorm at the time, were using a Ouija board to communicate with the poltergeist. No one knows for certain whether or not the spirts moved the planchette, but the next day, the students were astounded by the sight of paperclips floating near the windowsill. Suddenly, a pen and pencil flew across the room and hit the wall. That night, they were also frightened by a tapping sound coming from the outside of their window. The distraught students reported the paranormal incidents to the housing office.

One of the haunted fraternity houses on campus is the Phi Kappa Phi house. A member reported that one night, he was sleeping in his bedroom when he was awakened by the sensation that he was being forcibly held down. He had trouble breathing as well. After several seconds, he was finally able to move. He was covered with sweat as a result of his ordeal. This condition, known within the paranormal community, has been called "old hag syndrome." Many people experiencing pressure on their chest have attributed their discomfort to a sexual demon, an incubus or succubus. However, some psychologists refer to this phenomenon as "sleep paralysis," which sometimes occurs when people sleep on their backs.

In an article published in the October 30, 2014, edition of Troy's student newspaper, the *Tropolitan*, the author interviewed an alumnus, Matt Holmes, who told of a weird experience he had in McCartha Hall. One night, he and a friend decided to explore the building, which had assumed an aura of mystery because very few people were ever seen exiting. They had not gone far before something strange began happening. "Hallways seemed to change on us—sometimes slightly, like a picture or vent seemed to be in a different place than before, but sometimes even doors and whole corridors seemed to not be there when we would pass them again." Holmes admitted at the end of his story that he and his friend might have let their imaginations get the best of them.

Troy University might not be Alabama's most haunted campus, but the student body would argue that its ghosts are definitely some of the most active in the state's higher-education system.

### University of Alabama
### Tuscaloosa

The University of Alabama is the oldest public university in Alabama. In 1818, the federal government set aside a township in the Alabama Territory as the location for a "seminary of learning." The school was named the University of the State of Alabama on December 18, 1820. Tuscaloosa was chosen as the site of the university on December 29, 1827. The University of Alabama opened its doors in 1831, with fifty-two students and four professors. The curriculum included history, English grammar, mathematics, composition, and reading. The first president, Alva Woods, instituted strict rules of behavior that culminated in disciplinary problems. Following Woods' resignation in 1837, Pres. Basil Manly established a normal school, law school, and medical school. Landon G. Garland introduced military discipline to the university after he became president in 1855. In 1860, the student body became the Corps of Cadets. They helped defend the town and university after Union general James H. Wilson arrived at Tuscaloosa on April 3, 1865. Eventually, the cadets were repelled, enabling Federal soldiers to burn the university. Only a few buildings, including the President's Mansion, Gorgas House, and observatory, were unharmed. Garland resigned in 1866, leaving the new president, Col. James Thomas Murfee, with the task of rebuilding the university. Alabama's 1867 Constitution replaced the board of trustees with a politicized board of regents. The governor and state senate reinstated the board of trustees in 1876. As the result of a petition, the board authorized the enrollment of women students in 1893.

The military system continued throughout the remainder of the nineteenth century. It was finally abolished in 1903. Between 1902 and 1911, Pres. John William Abercrombie raised entrance requirements. He also established summer-school programs for secondary teachers, in an effort to improve the quality of high-school education. During George H. Denny's tenure as president (1912-36), fourteen buildings were constructed, and enrollment increased to 5,000 students. In World War II, women constituted the majority of the student body because of the large number of men who were in the military. The influx of veterans who enrolled at the university on the GI Bill after the war resulted in the creation of temporary housing for more than 600 students. The university also added the School of Dentistry and the School of Nursing in the postwar years.

On June 11, 1963, the Alabama National Guard compelled Gov. George C. Wallace to step aside and allow two black students, Vivian Malone and James Hood, to register for classes at the university. In 1969, the board of trustees established the University of Alabama System, which now included the University of Alabama at Birmingham and the University of Alabama in Huntsville. The emphasis in the 1990s was on improving research programs and economic development. In the early years of the twenty-first century, twenty new facilities were constructed. Alabama is known today not only for the quality of its academic programs but also for its varsity sports, especially the Crimson Tide football team. The University of Alabama focuses on preparing its students for the challenges of the future. However, the university's storied past reasserts itself through its ghost stories, which have been a vibrant part of campus life for decades.

One of the buildings that remained untouched by Gen. John Croxton's troops on April 3-4, 1865, was the sentry box, known today as Jason's Shrine. While the cadets were fighting the Federal troops outside of Tuscaloosa, two young men decided they were going to stay on campus and kill some Yankees. One of them hid inside the sentry box, and the other one walked around the campus, where the Yankees were burning all the buildings. He was standing outside the library, watching the soldiers burn books, when a burly sergeant asked him if he knew where they could get their hands on some whiskey. He replied, "Yes, sir. The cadets keep their whiskey in the sentry box." He guided the sergeant and two other soldiers to that location. He then threw the door open and stepped aside while the cadet hiding inside shot all three of them. Students say that late at night, you can still hear those Yankees rooting around the sentry box looking for their whiskey.

The most haunted building on campus is undoubtedly Smith Hall. Built in 1910, it was named after Dr. Eugene Allen Smith, who served the university as a professor of geology from 1871 to 1927. After Smith Hall was constructed, Dr. Smith moved his laboratory to the first floor, and he continued to work there for the next seventeen years. In 1955, Dr. Gary Hooks had his first encounter with Dr. Smith's ghost. He was working on his dissertation on the first floor late at night when he heard footsteps and muffled voices. Later, Hooks said that it sounded as if a group of students was being shown through the second-floor museum. In the early 1970s, several graduate students studying past midnight in Smith Hall heard an authoritative voice, like that of a teacher calling his class to order. The ghostly activity subsided for most of the 1970s and 1980s, but the number of paranormal incidents increased after the museum was added to the main floor. Several students and staff members have heard the rattling sound of the wooden wheels of Dr. Smith's carriage rolling around the floor and the clip-clop of horses' hooves late at night. One night, a group of students was studying inside Smith Hall when they heard the voices of what they thought were intruders. They followed the sound through the building to one particular classroom. When they opened the door, they were shocked to find that the desks and tables were scattered all over the room. Later, they learned that years before, a boiler exploded in the basement below this very room, killing a number of students. The basement itself has also been the site of paranormal activity. Students often report a feeling of being watched there. Late one afternoon, a young man working by himself in the lab was pushed into a closet by invisible hands. Whoever—or whatever—was responsible would not let him leave until the next morning.

The Gorgas House is one of only seven buildings to survive Croxton's Union troops' burning of the university. Built in 1829, the Gorgas House is the oldest building on campus. The plan was drawn up by architect William Nichols, who designed several buildings, including the state capitol at Tuscaloosa, the Old Capitol in Jackson, and the campus of the University of Mississippi in

*The clanking of Gen. Josiah Gorgas's sword has been heard on the staircase of the Gorgas House.* (Photo from en.wikipedia.org)

Oxford. The Gorgas House originally served as a dining hall and residence for the university steward. In the 1840s, it became a residence hall for faculty. Confederate general Josiah Gorgas and his wife, Amelia Gayle Gorgas, moved into the house after the Civil War. He also served as the seventh president of the University of Alabama until illness forced him to resign in 1870. Amelia, who was the daughter of Alabama governor John Gayle, worked as a librarian for the university. She and her daughters remained in the home until 1953. Today, the Gorgas House is a museum. For years, staff members and visitors have claimed to hear ghostly footsteps tread up the stairs, accompanied by the sound of a saber banging against the wall. General Gorgas, it seems, is still there in spirit.

## University of Montevallo
### Montevallo

The Alabama Girls' Industrial School opened its doors on October 13, 1896. It became a reality largely through the efforts of social reformer Julia Tutwiler, who promoted educational opportunities for women. The first president of the school was a local merchant named Henry Clay Reynolds. The faculty consisted of only eight members. The Olmsted Brothers, whose father designed New York's Central Park, planned the grounds.

The Main Residence Hall, built in 1897, was the first new building on campus. Reynolds Hall, constructed as part of the Montevallo Male Institute in 1851, served as the classroom building. The next president, Francis Marion Peterson, added wings to both halls.

The third president, Thomas Waverly Palmer, established a dairy on school grounds to give students experience in dairy farming. During his administration, the campus was expanded through the acquisition of several adjacent plots of land, including the Edmund King House. In 1919, the school changed its name to the Alabama Girls' Institute. Three years later, the phrase "College for Women" was added. The name was changed once again in 1923, this time to Alabama College, State College for Women, to reflect its status as a degree-granting institution.

In the 1920s, the school began preparing students for careers in education and home economics. Alabama College awarded its first BS degree in home economics in 1922. In 1925, Alabama became one of two states to offer programs in social work. The state's first speech clinic was opened at Alabama College in 1952.

In the early 1950s, enrollment declined so drastically that the administration decided to make Alabama College a coeducational institution. The first two male students enrolled in 1956. The college's first three African-American students—Ruby Kennebrew, Dorothy Turner, and Carolyn Buprop—were admitted in the fall of 1968. When the institution changed its name to the University of Montevallo on September 1, 1969, the school was divided into three colleges: Liberal Arts, Business, and Education. A fourth college— the College of Fine Arts—was added in 1973.

Student life is enriched by the university's men's and women's sports and by College Night, a three-day event dating back to 1919. The occasion ends with the performance of original one-act musicals. The university's beautiful white-columned buildings contain over a century's worth of memories and, according to students and faculty, a number of spirits as well.

Montevallo's most haunted building is the Main Residence Hall, a women's dormitory referred to by students as "Old Main." Some students call the dormitory "Buzzard Hall" because of the resemblance of the tangle of vines over the entranceway to buzzards' nests. The hall's most famous ghost story has its basis in fact. On February 4, 1908, Condie Cunningham was making hot chocolate over a little sterno heater. Somehow, the heater was knocked over, and the young woman's dressing ground caught fire. Instead of falling to the floor and rolling around, Condie ran screaming down the hallway, causing the flames to intensify. After a few horrific seconds, the poor girl collapsed in a smoldering heap at the top of the stairs. According to the local newspaper, Condie was taken to the hospital, where she died in agony several days later. A gentleman this writer interviewed at a Birmingham retirement center said that his mother attended the University of West Alabama at the time of Condie Cunningham's death. She told him that the odor of burning flesh was so strong that the dormitory was shut down for several days.

Dr. Frank McCoy, a former professor in the Art Department, said that Condie Cunningham has gained a second life in the stories that students tell about her. "Even today, you can talk to students who swear that Condie came into their room," he informed me. "She's been known to go into the shower and scream her head off. Some students have felt wind when the windows were closed. They have seen the carpet on the threshold ripple as if someone just walked into the room. Or they'll tell the story of a door opening, and there won't be anyone there. The girls say when she roams the halls, she doesn't do it quietly. She screams and runs through the halls as if she is still on fire. One young woman said that Condie is coming back because she is trying to live vicariously through the young students in the dorm." Students have also talked about windows opening and closing on their own. A few students have heard a disembodied female voice exclaiming, "Help me!"

The door to Condie Cunningham's room has also become the

*The ghost of a young woman who burned to death still races down the halls of Old Main.* (Photo from Wikimedia Commons)

subject of the dorm's ghost tales. The last time I visited Old Main in the early 2000s, the room was vacant. The RA told me that students refuse to stay in it because they hear screaming and talking at night. I was also told that students were "freaked out" by the door to the room because of the appearance of a screaming face in the grain of the wood. Dr. McCoy and I were escorted to a storage room in the basement, where the door was leaning against a wall. I suppose that, with a small dose of imagination, one could see the image of a face in the grain of the wood.

Reynolds Hall, now a theater building, is haunted by the ghost of its namesake, Capt. Henry Clay Reynolds. On March 31, 1865, he learned that General Wilson's army was preparing to attack the Brierfield Ironworks, a valuable smelting plant for the Confederacy. Dr. McCoy said that Reynolds was given the job of supervising Reynolds Hall, which had become a Confederate hospital. "He decided to go eight miles away to Brierfield and fight with the Confederate Army. Unfortunately, he left the wounded soldiers in Reynolds Hall unguarded, and when the Union Army came through, they massacred everyone in the hospital." Legend has it that Reynolds felt so guilty about abandoning his post that he never again left the hall. "I have been over to Reynolds on nights when maintenance people will swear that Reynolds' portrait in the entranceway has been moved," Dr. McCoy said. "They will take it down, and it will move back to its proper place. No one has ever been caught moving it, but it does in fact move around the building. Every now and then, a gust of wind will blow across the stage when the doors aren't open, so it's very easy to imagine that there's someone else in the room." In addition, Reynolds' blue apparition is said to wander through the hall. Windows and doors open and shut by themselves, and cold spots pop up in parts of the building.

*Capt. Henry Clay Reynolds' guilt-ridden apparition has been seen inside Reynolds Hall.* (Photo from Wikimedia Commons)

The most incongruous-looking building on campus is the Edmund King House, a mansion built in 1823 by Edmund King. He was a wealthy merchant who came to the area to trade with the Indians. King was very proud of his fruit orchard behind the mansion. It is said that when he was an old man, he would take walks through the orchard and the little cemetery where his beloved wife, Nancy, is buried. King's twenty-one-year-old son was accidentally shot by one of his brothers while hunting deer, and he is also buried there. According to legend, King was in his orchard in 1863 when a tree limb fell on his head, killing him. For many years, people have seen his ghost walking through the orchard with a lantern and shovel. He is supposedly trying to dig up the gold he buried there when the Yankees arrived at Montevallo in 1865. According to Dr. McCoy, money is the reason for King's frenzied activity inside the mansion. "The story goes that King's ghost will show up periodically in one of the upstairs windows, where you can see him counting his money. At times, he will lose money or cannot figure out why his books won't balance, and he starts roaming the inside of the house." Years after King's death, his children and grandchildren often heard the sound of someone rising from the bed and crossing the room. The strangest tale associated with the house is the story of a wedding feast. As a groomsman was carving a roast pig, a "huge white thing" crept from beneath the table, hovered between the bride and groom for an instant, and then vanished. Reports of paranormal activity in the building continue to this day. The house is now used for university functions, and occasionally, a strange light is seen floating behind the mansion. In the early 2000s, one young couple said an elderly man dressed in nineteenth-century clothes appeared in an upstairs window and waved at them.

Named after Thomas Waverly Palmer, Palmer Hall is the setting for the university's College Night. Dr. McCoy said that the Smithsonian Institution recognized College Night as having the longest-running student-produced and student-directed show in the United States. "It is a very intense rivalry. Students declare that they are gold or purple—the school's colors. Then they go through

*The ghost of Edmund King has been seen counting his money in his bedroom on the second floor of the King House.* (Photo from Wikimedia Commons)

various athletic competitions, followed by debates. Each group writes, produces, choreographs, and acts in a production it has written. Then on Saturday, a winner is declared. Probably no more than ten days a year do students have an interest in Palmer, but during that time, the rivalry and intense emotion are raucous in Palmer Hall." The ghost of Prof. W. H. Trumbauer, known affectionately as "Trummy," haunts the building. As Trumbauer was an ardent supporter of College Night, his ghost is probably upset because he was not listed as one of the designers of Palmer Hall on the cornerstone. After he died, Trummy decided to get even, "not in a malicious way, but more in keeping with the spirit of College Night, which is intense but fun," Dr. McCoy said. "Trummy will wander backstage and appear and disappear as students are getting ready. Most of these students have never appeared on stage before and certainly not in front of 1,100 people with bands playing and

*Trummy's ghost still chooses the best play during College Night.* (Photo from Wikimedia Commons)

cheerleaders, so the fact that they would see an apparition below the stage is understandable. Every once in a while, he gets really mischievous. He determines the outcome of the competition by spinning the battens over the performance he likes best." A young woman practicing the organ in Palmer Hall one evening may have made contact with the old professor. She stopped playing and was preparing to go home when she heard a spectral voice ask her to play some more. Students getting ready in the dressing room claim to have seen the figures of women wearing long dresses in the old mirrors.

## University of North Alabama
### Florence

The Methodist Church founded LaGrange College, the precursor of the University of North Alabama, near Leighton in 1830. The school began with seventy male students and three faculty members. The first president was Rev. Robert Paine.

After Richard Henderson Rivers became president in 1854, the campus of LaGrange College was moved fifteen miles away to Florence. One year later, the name of the school was changed to Florence Wesleyan University. The school barely managed to remain open during the Civil War and closed down by 1866.

Florence Wesleyan University reopened in 1868, but its efforts to attract new students were ineffective. In 1870, the state of Alabama acquired the struggling university from the North American Methodist Conference. The name was changed to the State Normal School at Florence in accordance with the agreement drawn up with the Methodist Conference.

In 1874, the school became one of the nation's first coeducational teachers' colleges when it admitted thirty-one female students. The Alabama State Board of Education took over the university in 1911. Between 1914 and 1922, the school experienced a period of vigorous growth that necessitated the construction of two new dormitories.

A laboratory elementary school, Kilby Training School, opened on the campus in 1922. By 2016, it was Alabama's only university-owned elementary school. After the institution's name was changed to Florence State Teachers College in 1929, a gymnasium, Bibb Graves Hall, married-student housing, Rogers Hall, and the Memorial Amphitheater were constructed.

The school became Florence State College in 1957. Between 1957 and 1958, more buildings were added, including the Floyd Science Building and Student Union Building. In 1963, Wendell Wilkie Gunn became the first black student admitted to the school.

Sororities and fraternities were established on the campus in 1972. In 1974, the school's name was changed once again, this time to the University of North Alabama. Several buildings were renovated after Robert L. Potts became president in 1990, despite the fact that the university was experiencing financial setbacks.

In 2005, the university started the UNA Honors Program. One

of the school's most popular events is the George Lindsey UNA Film Festival. Football and baseball have been athletic mainstays at the university since 1911.

The off-campus bookstore is said to be haunted. It was built as a private residence in the early 1900s by a well-to-do merchant from Florence. He and his wife had tried for years to have a child and had almost given up when little Mollie was born. She instantly became the apple of her father's eye. He soon made a habit of bringing her a little present every day when he returned from work.

One day, the merchant brought home a box with holes in it. Mollie ran down the sidewalk to greet her dad and asked him what was inside the box. She opened the lid, and there was a little puppy.

Mollie and her pet hit it off right away and soon became inseparable. One hot August day, Mollie was playing outside with her puppy when she decided to go inside and take a nap. She was halfway up the stairs when the puppy started scratching and biting the backs of her legs. Her screams alerted her mother, who grabbed Mollie and carried her upstairs to wash her wounds. It turned out that her puppy was rabid, and the poor little girl died in agony.

The house changed many times over the years. In 1970, the University of North Alabama bought the home, and it was taken over by a fraternity. After the boys lived there a while, they made some drastic changes, knocking out walls and adding a room.

It was not long before strange things started happening. Some nights, when the frat boys sat downstairs after dinner to talk or study, they would hear a dog barking upstairs. Several times, they ran upstairs to catch the dog, but they never found him.

More than once, the boys were awakened at night by the sound of a child crying. They jumped out of bed and searched the house for the child but found nothing. That fall, during homecoming, the queen and her court were on a balcony watching the parade below when they saw a girl and a dog on the lawn. Because the child was wearing an old-fashioned dress, they assumed she had wandered off one of the floats. The girls ran downstairs and caught sight of the girl and the dog walking around the corner of the house. As soon as they rounded the corner, they could not see the girl. It was as if she had just vanished into thin air.

That summer, after school was out, a man was hired to look after the house. He was walking down the street one day when he saw a little girl sitting on the curb in front of the house. He went over to her and asked if she was lost. She said, "Oh, no. I live here." She then walked up the sidewalk, climbed up the steps to the front porch, and walked right through the bolted door. Strange things still occur at the off-campus bookstore. Although Mollie and her dog have not been seen in years, she still makes her presence known by periodically snatching candy from a shelf.

Wesleyan Hall, the oldest building on campus, was designed by Adolphys Heiman and constructed by Zebulon Pike Morrison in 1856. During the Civil War, the castle-like building was instrumental in saving Florence from complete destruction. According to legend, when General Sherman's army arrived in Florence, he agreed to spare the city if he was allowed to use Wesleyan Hall as his headquarters. For over a century, a reminder of Sherman's stay in Florence could be found in the main stairway. Legend has it that a Yankee sergeant got drunk and rode his horse up the staircase, leaving indentations of horseshoes on the steps that were clearly visible until they were covered up by rubber coasters.

Wesleyan Hall is said to be haunted by the ghost of a drummer boy named Jeremiah whose father was a colonel in Sherman's army. One day, the boy's waterlogged corpse was found floating in Cedar Creek near One Lane Bridge. Some people said Jeremiah was kidnapped and murdered, while others believed he either fell off the bridge accidentally or committed suicide. The boy's sodden apparition has been sighted standing in the hallways or on the front lawn of Wesleyan Hall in the moonlight. Some students and staff members have heard a spectral voice, ghostly footsteps, and the bouncing of a ball. Students sitting in class have been overcome with chills. One day, a young man scoffed at the stories of the ghostly drummer boy haunting the hallways. During class, he fell violently to the floor. As his classmates helped him back to his seat, he said it felt as though

*The ghost of a drowned drummer boy makes his presence known in Wesleyan Hall.* (Photo from Wikimedia Commons)

someone had kicked him in the back. Students taking classes at Wesleyan Hall have learned to take its ghost stories seriously.

In 1830, an aspiring entrepreneur named John Simpson built the beautiful mansion at 472 North Court Street. He amassed a fortune in the mercantile and land-speculation business. His wife, Margaret, turned her beloved home into the social center of Florence. She was said to be a perfectionist who made sure that everything was in its place before guests arrived for her lavish parties.

In 1990, David Brubaker donated the house to the university for use as the admissions office. Today, the old home bears the name of Brubaker's wife, Coby. Margaret Simpson's ghost is said to patrol the halls, looking for irregularities in the furnishings. She expresses her displeasure if anything is not quite right, especially when weddings are held there. Jessica Penot, author of *Haunted North Alabama*, tells the story of a woman who was in the basement, preparing for a wedding, when she heard chairs banging around

*Margaret Simpson's fastidious spirit lets it be known when she disapproves of the furnishings in Coby Hall.* (Photo from Wikimedia Commons)

above her. Initially, she was not concerned because she assumed that the caterers had arrived and were setting up. Her mood changed drastically, however, when she walked upstairs and discovered that she was the only one inside the house.

## University of West Alabama
### Livingston

Webb Hall, the first female dormitory on the campus of Livingston Female Academy, was built in 1895. It was named for R. D. Webb, who served on the board of trustees for many years. In addition to the dorm rooms, the building contained a kitchen and dining room. Following a devastating fire on April 3, 1909, damages were estimated at $10,000. When word spread that most of the students had lost all of their possessions, residents of Livingston raised over two hundred dollars to purchase books, clothes, and school supplies. A few families allowed students to stay in their homes. Webb Hall was rebuilt in 1911 through the issuing of interest-bearing bonds. The dormitory burned down a second time in 1914 and was rebuilt in 1915. By the 1960s, the only women living in the dormitory were unmarried female professors. At the end of the 1970s, Webb Hall was converted into the administration building. Today, it houses the Office of the President, the Office of the Provost, the Registrar's Office, the Business Office, and, according to some students and administrators, the spirit of one of the old dormitory's former residents.

Suspicions that Webb Hall might be haunted were raised in the late 1960s. Between 1969 and 1971, university athletes stayed in the old dorm rooms during Christmas and Easter break. "We all heard the sound of people talking and moving around the hallway," Stan

*Webb Hall, the first female dormitory on the campus of the University of West Alabama, was built in 1895. It burned in 1909 and was rebuilt in 1911. The dormitory burned a second time in 1914 and was rebuilt in 1915. (Photo by Alan Brown)*

Nerewski, one of those athletes, told me. "When we opened our bedroom doors and looked out, there was no one there."

Webb Hall's reputation as a haunted building became known campus-wide in 1993. George Snow, the comptroller, was staying late one spring night, just as he had done many nights before, when he had an encounter of the paranormal kind. "It was probably 7:00 or 7:30," he told me. "I got to the point that I was quitting for the day. Security had already been around. Now, there's a short hall outside of my office that runs right next to a long hall. We got one security light at the far end of this hall and nothing on the side hall. I had just locked the door and gone out. And when I got to this door in the hallway, off to my right, I heard a rustling sound that sounded for all the world like a woman in multiple petticoats from the late part of the last century. When I heard that, I got out of there. I went through the door and turned a light on quick. There was nothing there. Within the next two weeks on three different occasions, I smelled lilac perfume, an old scent that women used to wear years ago."

The spectral student manifested again in 2006. Lawson Edmonds, the purchasing agent for the university, detected the unmistakable scent of lilac perfume in the same area where George Snow had his ghostly experience. "During Christmas break that year, I smelled the perfume for five days in a row," Edmonds told me. "The smell usually appears when the building has been closed for a while, like on weekends or during breaks. When this happens, the hair rises up on my arms. A few years ago, I brought my daughter and three of her friends to the Business Office during Christmas break, and they smelled the perfume as well. I hadn't told anyone about it at the time."

Poltergeist activity has also occurred in Webb Hall. Teresa Biglane, an advisor in the Financial Aid Office, told me that on October 31, 2006, she and a secretary were talking about the ghost tour that had been given in town the night before. "Suddenly, the toilet in the bathroom in back of the office flushed by itself. I thought it might have been a coincidence, so we started talking again, and right after I said the word 'ghost,' the toilet flushed again. We decided to change the subject, and nothing strange happened that afternoon."

*Comptroller George Snow sensed the presence of a female student from the turn of the century in the hallway outside his office.* (Photo by Alan Brown)

A work-study who also went on the ghost tour wanted to conduct her own investigation of Webb Hall. Using her key to the front door, she and her friends entered and made their way to the Business Office on the second floor. They sat down in a circle at the end of hallway. One of them placed a Ouija board on the floor, and the girls placed their fingers on the planchette. One of them asked, "Is there a ghost here?" and the planchette moved to the "yes" square. They were unable to elicit any more responses from the spirit that night.

The Printing Department on the first floor also seems to be haunted. Michelle Hagood, who has worked in Printing since 2010, has had what appears to be an encounter with the unknown. "I used to work in the back of the Printing Department," she told me. "This was between 2011 and 2014. I had an *L*-shaped table back in a little corner. There were many nights that I had to stay late, and it would be very quiet. Then all of a sudden, all heck would break loose. The first night it happened, I packed up and left. It sounded like there was someone or something behind me, and I know there wasn't. There was nothing but empty space. At that time, there was a shelving unit that we kept our jobs in, and it was firmly attached to the wall, so it wasn't something that you could go behind or even a mouse. Even a mouse does not make that noise. And it only happened late at night. It was more of a slamming, stomping kind of a noise. It was loud enough to startle. It wasn't this cute, tiny little noise that just grew. It still gives me goosebumps. And it was right behind me. I'd look, and there was a wall right there. Now, mind you, there was a hallway on the other side of the wall. But at 9:00-10:00 at night, there's nobody in the building. And even if a police officer was walking the hallway, he would have no reason to do that. And it would happen at odd times. There are certain times of the year when I get really busy, and it's usually after commencement. I can't tell you the season. And I don't work back there anymore. I worked back there for maybe four years, and I heard it maybe five times while I was back there. It would happen at different times. The sound was usually the same, but it was never in the same spot. It gave me the chills. It was not a happy sound. I've worked in lots of buildings late, and I've never

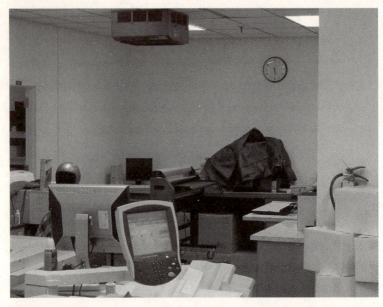

*Between 2011 and 2014, Michelle Hagood heard strange sounds late at night in the Printing Department.* (Photo by Alan Brown)

heard anything like this before. I like it quiet, so I don't have music on, and we don't have an air-conditioning unit on. It was dead quiet. It did not make me feel comfortable."

Another ghostly incident occurred at Webb Hall in 2013. A young man who served as a university escort was walking a young lady back to her dormitory at 10:00 P.M. When they reached Webb Hall, the young lady exclaimed, "Look! There's a girl staring out the window." He looked in the direction where she was pointing and saw a blonde girl in a white dress standing in a window of the second floor. A few seconds later, the entity vanished.

The sightings at Webb Hall have led some people to conjecture that at least one resident perished in the two fires that destroyed the dormitory. So far, research in the University Archives has produced no evidence that anyone died in Webb Hall in 1909 or 1914. However, the absence of tangible proof that someone died there a century ago has not discouraged students from entertaining themselves late at night in the dorms by telling stories about the ghost of Webb Hall.

Selden Hall was built in 1968 as a residence hall for 194 students. It was named after Armistead Selden, Jr., who served as U.S. ambassador to Fiji, Tonga, Western Samoa, and New Zealand. He also served in the Alabama House of Representatives from 1951 to 1952 and in the U.S. Congress from 1953 to 1969. The students living in the coed dorm do not have kitchens or bathrooms in their rooms. However, they have a great ghost story that has been passed down to incoming freshmen for decades.

A number of the dorm's ghost stories were published on October 24, 1982, in the *Livingston Life*. In the article titled "Every Day Is Halloween with Octavia," Kim Brown recounted the encounters she and other students had with the "resident ghost" named "Octavia" in Selden Hall. The first story took place in the winter of 1981 during final-exam week. Kim and her roommate, Angela, were studying hard in their fourth-floor room when they decided to go to a local restaurant named Dandy Don's for a snack. Kim distinctly remembered that they had left the stereo and all of the lights on. The curtains and window were open as well. After the girls finished their cheeseburgers at Dandy Don's, Kim parked her car beside the dorm, and she and Angela began walking up the sidewalk to Selden. The girls had just passed the gingko tree in front of Speith Hall when Kim happened to glance up at their dorm room. She was wondering why she was unable to see the air-conditioning vent on the far wall of their room when, suddenly, she realized that someone was standing in the window looking down at her and her roommate. As the girls walked on, they could make out the facial features of their uninvited visitor. She was a short young woman with long, blonde hair and white skin. "The white of her jersey, her hair, and her skin were so nearly the same shade that they were barely distinguishable," Kim said. She clearly remembered the blood-red sleeves of the university baseball jersey she wore. However, the girl's most striking feature was her face, which Kim described as a "white blank." She grabbed her roommate's arm to get her attention. All Angela said was, "I know." As the girls watched in stunned silence, the apparition turned and floated out of sight.

Kim and Angela ran up the stairs to the fourth floor, fully expecting to find their room ransacked by the intruder. The room was exactly as they had left it. Angela had taken only a few steps into the room when she was overcome by what she called a "force pushing out of the walls and pushing in" on her. At the same moment, Kim felt chills crawl up her spine. The girls ran down the hall and brought their friend Dana to the room because she was the "level-headed one." Dana was skeptical when she entered, but she soon admitted to feeling cold as well. Once the "creepy" feeling subsided, Dana shared a ghostly experience she had had earlier in the quarter. One afternoon, she returned to her room after class and was about to open the door when she heard her desk drawers, closets, and window slam shut. She also heard the light switch clicking off and on. Once she had summoned up the courage to enter the room, she found that the closet doors she had left open were shut and the window she had left closed was open.

The girls christened their spectral visitor "Octavia," after a photograph Kim had seen in a baby names book. When they talked to Vice President James Horner about Octavia, he informed them that he had received a large number of reports of haunted activity in Selden over the years. Over the previous summer, a girl was in her third-floor room studying on her bed when she noticed the figure of a faceless young woman staring at her from outside the window. The girl was so terrified by the apparition that she moved out of the room the next day. Other students living in Selden have heard spectral knocks that come out of nowhere late at night and high-heeled footsteps on the upper floors. The steps start at a specific spot, walk the full length of the hall, and start again at the original place.

Octavia's presence has been felt by Selden residents in the twenty-first century as well. In 2010, a female student was in Room 207 waiting for a friend to come back from class. She walked out of the room after a few minutes, shut the door, and went to the community

*Students have reported seeing the ghost of a student named Octavia in an upper window of Selden Hall.* (Photo by Alan Brown)

bathroom. When she returned, she tried to open the door, but it felt as if someone was pushing against it from the other side. The pressure diminished after a few minutes, and the girl was able to open the door. No one was in the room. A male student had a similar experience in Selden Hall the same year. One morning, he left the door to his room open and walked down to the community bathroom to take a shower. When he walked back into his room, the door suddenly slammed shut with a loud "bang!" He quickly opened the door; the hallway was completely empty.

Selden Hall's ghost story has evolved over the years. By the 2000s, she had become a nameless phantom who either committed suicide or was murdered in the dorm. Real or not, she lives on in the tales told by upperclassmen to initiate freshmen into the scary aspects of college life.

The most haunted building on campus is undoubtedly the Julia Tutwiler Library. Built in 1960, it appears to have been ghost-free until 1995, when a graduate student and ex-marine named Ray Jordan fell asleep in one of the back rooms on the first floor while studying for a final exam. When he woke up at 11:00 P.M., the night librarian, Becky Babb, was turning off the lights. By the time Ray got to the front desk, Becky had locked the door and driven away. While he was standing by the circulation desk, he began hearing the sounds of bookshelves being bumped and books being slammed shut. Suddenly, Ray felt the presence of someone else. "I realized I wasn't in the library alone," Ray told me. "I could tell where it was without seeing it. I was really scared at that point." Ray walked into the back office, where his fear intensified. "I was standing there, and I realized that something was right by me, and that was when my hair almost fell out. [A few seconds later], it walked behind me. There was this really cool breeze that went by with it, and then [the entity] stopped by a bookshelf there in the office." Once Ray regained his composure, he returned to the circulation desk, called the Security Office, and asked one of the officers to come over to the library and let him out.

*Since 1995, a patron and librarian have reported paranormal activity inside the Julia Tutwiler Library.* (Photo by Alan Brown)

*Staff working late at night have heard footsteps and books falling from shelves on the second floor when, supposedly, it was empty.* (Photo by Alan Brown)

*A librarian standing behind the circulation desk late in the evening has been touched by spectral fingers.* (Photo by Alan Brown)

The librarian, Becky, has also had a number of weird experiences in the library between 9:00 and 11:00. Most of the disturbances take the form of sounds on the second floor, such as footsteps or books falling off a shelf. On one occasion, one of the spirits got "up close and personal" with Becky. She was standing behind the circulation desk when she felt fingers run across her back and down her arm. The most frightening incident occurred in 2011. Becky was getting ready to close up when she heard a squeaking sound coming from the second floor, which was supposed to be empty at the time. She crept up the stairs and was surprised to see an antique wheelchair right by the top step. Normally, the wheelchair is kept inside a locked meeting room. Becky was so frightened that she ran back downstairs, locked the door, and left.

Ghost-hunting groups have conducted investigations at the library in recent years. One group was filming inside the Alabama Room—the archives—in total darkness with a night-vision camera. When they examined the footage, they could clearly see an orb flit across the screen. Thinking that the camera might have captured a flying insect, the members searched the room, but no bugs could be found.

# Chapter 3
# Haunted Buildings

### Bryce Hospital
### Tuscaloosa

In 1852, plans were made to build a hospital for the mentally ill on land once owned by Mims Jemison, a member of one of Alabama's wealthiest families. Advocates of the new hospital were 1830s activists Dorothea Dix and Thomas Story Kirkbride. Architect Samuel Sloan was hired to design the hospital in the Italianate style, using the Kirkbride Plan as his guide. Construction began in 1853. When the hospital was completed in 1859, it became the first building in Tuscaloosa with central heating and gas lighting. The Alabama Insane Hospital opened its doors two years later. Dix advocated hiring Peter Bryce from South Carolina as the first superintendent because of his reformist ideas. The hospital was later renamed for him. Not only did Bryce demand that his patients be treated with kindness, respect, and understanding, but he also dispensed with the use of shackles and straitjackets in 1882. He even encouraged the patients to print their own newspaper, *The Meteor*, in the 1880s. Patients were taught such useful skills as sewing. Bryce Hospital was nearly self-sufficient, with its own laundry, dairy, and bakery.

In the twentieth century, the quality of patient care declined steadily as the number of patients increased. When Gov. Lurleen Wallace visited Bryce Hospital in 1967, she was so moved by the plight of a little girl who called her "Mama!" that she lobbied to generate more funds for the facility. After the cigarette tax for mental-health treatment was cut in 1970, the hospital staff was drastically reduced. Patients slept on urine-soaked beds or on the floor. Many of the hospital's 5,200 patients suffered from abuse and neglect. An article in the *Montgomery Advertiser* compared the facility to a Nazi concentration camp. The deplorable conditions at Bryce Hospital became widely known in 1970 during a court case that involved a fifteen-year-old boy named Ricky Wyatt, who had been committed to the mental hospital even though he had displayed no signs of mental illness. The case led to federal standards for hospital care of the mentally ill across the nation. In 2009, Gov. Bob Riley announced the takeover of Bryce Hospital by the University of Alabama, which pledged millions of dollars to take care of the environmental problems on the 180-acre site and restore the main building. For now, Bryce Hospital sits empty, home to nothing more than bad memories and, some say, the ghosts of its former patients.

Bryce Hospital's reputation as one of the state's most haunted sites is the product of reports by hundreds of witnesses. Trespassers claim to have heard strange noises, such as the ringing of telephones and intercom calls to doctors, the sound of disembodied footsteps, and the scraping of furniture across the floors of vacant rooms. Cold spots appear throughout the old building. Several visitors have been scratched by unseen hands.

One of the best-known ghost stories from the Bryce Hospital campus involves a boy between seven and eight years old. One day, he was placed in a vat of freezing water during a hydrotherapy session. As soon as his feet touched the water, the boy began kicking and screaming. The orderlies pushed his head under the water; one minute later, his struggling ceased. The boy was dead. Many people claim to have seen the specter of a little blonde boy wearing pants with suspenders and a shabby coat. Over the years, visitors with a "soft spot" have left small toys in the hydrotherapy room for him to play with. Teenagers who have ventured out to the site claim to have been chased by a tall man in a black coat.

Today, Bryce Hospital is an abandoned, graffiti-covered hulk, its former grandeur eroded by neglect and the passage of time. The No Trespassing signs and the threat of arrest seem to have done little to deter the legions of ghost hunters bent on collecting definitive evidence of the existence of the paranormal.

## Fort Conde Inn
## Mobile

Edward Hall came to Mobile in the 1820s with the goal of making a fortune buying Alabama cotton and selling it on the lucrative European market. He was a very driven man who started out as a commission merchant and branched out, becoming one of the founders of the Bank of Mobile in 1823. He threw his hat in the political ring in the 1840s, serving as mayor of Mobile in 1840-41.

In the 1830s, Hall decided to build a house befitting his status as one of the city's most successful businessmen. On December 31, 1834, he paid $800 for the lot on which he was to build his mansion. The land was part of Mobile's earliest settlements. Fort Conde was built by the French in 1720 to prevent attacks by the British and Spanish. It was named after the Prince of Condé, Louis Henri Joseph de Bourbon. In 1853, Isaac Spears purchased the house.

A widow named Ellen Quinn became the next owner in 1896. She then deeded the house to her daughter, Mamie, who married Thomas Joseph Ford. Their only son, Thomas Allison Ford, Sr., had three sons with his wife, Mabel: Thomas Allison Ford, Jr., Michael Aloysius Ford, Sr., and Richard Vincent Ford. Members of the Ford family continued living in the home for most of the twentieth century.

The family sold the house at 165 St. Emanuel Street to the city of Mobile, which had been redeveloping Fort Conde Village since 1976. The city installed gas lamps and bricked the streets. In 1990, the owner of the Fort Conde Restoration Venture, Lawrence Posner, and his business partner, David Bradley, began restoring eleven buildings in the district, one of which became the Fort Conde Inn, a bed and breakfast. Before the inn opened on June 29, 2011, doors and window sashes were repaired. In addition, the parlors were restored to their original dimensions, and the main stair railing and newel posts were re-milled. All of the improvements were made in accordance with Edward Hall's original specifications.

The Hall-Ford house is the second-oldest building in Mobile, as well as one of the city's finest examples of early-nineteenth-century residences. The house's Greek Revival style was melded with the raised "Creole cottage" building type. The main building is constructed of brick covered with smooth stucco. Light Doric columns were placed on the front porches, whose walls are made of plaster. Two stuccoed brick chimneys were built on the north and south sides of the house. A centrally located chimney was superimposed on each service wing. The iron fence encircling the house was added in the 1870s or 1880s.

The interior follows the typical plan for early-nineteenth-century houses: a central hall with two rooms on each side. The main stairway at the rear of the hall consists of a double flight on each floor. The floors were made with random-width pine boards. Painted plaster coats the walls and ceilings.

The Fort Conde Inn is on several lists of the most haunted hotels in Alabama. According to the Shadowlands website, guests and staff hear disembodied voices when the bed and breakfast is empty. Some guests have sensed an unnerving presence on the second floor. Ghost-hunting groups have detected as many as seven separate entities inside the inn. One of these groups—ANR Paranormal—visited the Fort Conde Inn on September 6, 2013. They began their investigation with an EVP session on the second floor. The members of the group were sitting around a table when one of their EMF meters lit up. At the same moment, one of the investigators felt chills. A few minutes later, one of the investigators asked, "Did you hear that?" Almost instantly, the recorders captured a female voice saying, "It's working." The director of the group, James Rosier, Jr., asked, "Can you see us?" The spirit box responded, "Yes." When Rosier asked, "In what year did you die?" the box replied, "I didn't." The investigators then switched over to a P-SB7 spirit box and asked, "Is this box better for you?" A voice responded, "A little." When asked to whom the group was speaking, the spirit box replied, "Ford."

All of the rooms at the Fort Conde Inn have a "supernatural

*A desk clerk saw the shadow of a person floating on the second-floor landing at the Fort Conde Inn.* (Courtesy Marilyn Brown)

feel." Strange noises have been reported throughout the bed and breakfast. Desk clerks who spend the night in a room on the third floor have heard footsteps going up and down the stairs. Maids have found the indentations of bodies on beds where no one was sleeping the night before.

Amanda McBride, a desk clerk at the Fort Conde Inn, told me that she observed something unusual when she was walking down the stairs one morning. "I saw the shadow of a person floating in front of the little white shelf on the second-floor landing. I told the cook about the shadow, and he said, 'Oh, you mean the lady on the landing.'"

Amanda had another strange encounter when she was sitting at her desk on the first floor. "I was typing and, in the corner of my eye, I saw a white shape. I bent my head down and prayed over it. When I looked back, it was gone. At the time, I blamed it on the mirror in the corner of the room, but I don't think it was it."

### Fort Morgan
### Gulf Shores

Fort Morgan was actually the second fort to be built on Mobile Bay. The first, Fort Bowyer, was erected on Mobile Point in 1813 in anticipation of attacks by the British during the War of 1812. It was named after Col. John Bowyer, who completed its construction. Forces consisting of British Marines and Creek Indians waged their first attack against the log-and-sand structure on September 15, 1814. The American forces prevailed, sinking the HMS *Hermes* and forcing the British and Creeks to retreat. The defenders of Fort Bowyer were vastly outnumbered in their next encounter with the British and surrendered in early February 1815. Under the terms of the treaty that ended the War of 1812, the British were compelled to return Fort Bowyer to the U.S. Thirty-two British soldiers and four American soldiers died during the two attacks on the fort.

Fort Morgan, a pentagonal structure with five bastions and a citadel, was designed by Simon Bernard, who had served as a military engineer under Napoleon. Following Bernard's death from yellow fever, Samuel Hopkins was hired as a replacement, but he died without making much progress. The third contractor was Capt. R. E. DeRussey of the Army Corps of Engineers. For the most part, he used slaves to build the fort. A contractor was Capt. R. E. DeRussey of the Army Corps of Engineers. For the most part, he used slaves to build the fort. After Captain DeRussey became ill in 1825, Lt. Cornelius Ogden supervised the construction of Fort Morgan, which was completed in 1834. The project cost more money and took more time to complete because of the army's determination to stick to Bernard's original plan. The post was named after Revolutionary War hero Daniel Morgan. At the time, Fort Morgan was widely hailed as one of the finest examples of military architecture in the world. Company B of the Second Artillery assumed control of Fort Morgan until being called to duty during the Second Seminole War. Between 1836 and 1837, a large group of Creek Indians were briefly incarcerated at Fort Morgan before continuing their forced evacuation of their homeland on the Trail of Tears. Eighty Creeks died during their internment.

After 1842, Fort Morgan was not fully garrisoned until January 3, 1861, when four companies of Alabama volunteers under the command of Col. John B. Todd captured it. Immediately, an earthwork water battery was built to strengthen the fort. Eighteen of the fort's most powerful guns were positioned facing the Main Ship Channel directly across from the fort to provide protection for blockade runners entering Mobile Bay. In addition, a series of mines called "torpedoes" was placed in the channel. Fort Morgan's defenses were so formidable, in fact, that no Union forces dared to attack it until August 5, 1864, when Adm. David G. Farragut's fleet of four ironclads and several wooden ships waged an all-out assault on the fort. Under the battle cry "Damn the torpedoes! Full steam ahead!" Farragut led his forces past Fort Morgan and into Mobile Bay after capturing the *Tennessee* and *Selma* and sinking the *Gaines*. Farragut then captured Fort Gaines, enabling his land forces to fire on Fort

Morgan on August 9. After being heavily bombarded on August 22, Fort Morgan finally surrendered on August 23. The fort's commander, Richard L. Page, spiked the fort's guns before raising the white flag. Approximately 1,800 men died during the siege.

In the 1870s, Fort Morgan was upgraded with the installation of twelve Parrott rifles. Shortly afterward, the War Department abandoned the fort, though it was reactivated in 1898 during the Spanish-American War. Several wooden buildings were constructed at this time, including the Administration Building, which cost $2,379. Between 1895 and 1900, the secretary of war, William Endicott, ordered the construction of five concrete batteries, complete with electricity and communication capabilities. During the Spanish-American War, the fort was equipped with eight ten-inch smoothbore cannon that had been modified with rifled barrel sleeves.

Changes made in the old fort in the twentieth century were necessitated by the rigors of nature and demands of modern warfare. The hurricanes of 1906 and 1916 heavily damaged the wooden houses along Officers' Row. In 1916, battleships fired on a 10-inch gun mounted on a disappearing carriage inside the fort to test its durability. In 1917, shortly after the U.S. entered World War I, soldiers received training with anti-aircraft batteries at Fort Morgan. The war also brought a Morse code transmitting and receiving station to the fort. Two British 9.2-inch howitzers were installed in 1920 but were removed a year later. The fort was deactivated in 1923 and put in caretaker status. In 1941, Fort Morgan was mustered into service once again and operated throughout World War II. It was manned by Battery F, Fiftieth Coast Artillery Corps, Navy, and Coast Guard units. The U.S. Army built an adjacent airfield in 1947. The army fortified the structure with the installation of two Model 1918 155mm guns on top of the fort and three more guns on the parade grounds. The state of Alabama acquired Fort Morgan in 1946. In 1950, the U.S. Artillery Corps was disbanded. Fort Morgan was designated as a National Historical Landmark in 1960. Today, Fort Morgan stands as a portal into America's military past and, some say, into the paranormal as well.

By the very nature of its history, Fort Morgan stimulates the imaginations of employees and visitors. Sandy Powell and her husband, Tom, have been visiting it for years. They have not had any paranormal experiences inside the fort, but they admit that the place is "spooky." "People died and suffered there," Sandy said. "Anyplace you go where people died, it makes it spooky. I think it could be haunted. I wouldn't want to stay there at night." Winnie McIntosh, who is in charge of admissions at Fort Morgan, said that some visitors have reported having a very "creepy" feeling there. "They come in and say, 'I had an experience. I can feel them.'" Speaking for herself, Winnie has never been frightened inside Fort Morgan, even as a child.

Nevertheless, a large number of eyewitnesses to paranormal events have surfaced over the years. Not surprisingly, the earliest ghost stories date back to the Civil War. According to local lore, a bomb exploded in a room, killing a number of men. Supposedly, their screams still echo through the casements at night. Approximately thirty years later, an unidentified man raped and beat a woman to death inside the abandoned fort. The woman has become a revenant, endlessly wandering around Fort Morgan in search of her assailant. The final violent incident that has generated ghostly tales occurred in 1916 or 1917 when a prisoner hanged himself inside his jail cell. His spectral form has been sighted numerous times over the years.

However, much of the fort's paranormal activity cannot be traced back to a specific historic incident. Many visitors claim to have been overcome by a feeling of dread, usually before the appearance of a soldier wearing a tattered Confederate uniform. People have also seen—and photographed—strange mists and luminous orbs. Visitors have heard moans and cries in the prison area. Disembodied voices have been known to disrupt the tranquility of Fort Morgan. Shadowy figures that manifest at the fort have been misidentified as members of tour groups. Several years ago, a woman entered a dimly lit room and encountered what she thought was her group. When her eyes became accustomed to the darkness, she realized that the people in the room were actually phantom soldiers moving around. The woman turned around and rejoined her tour group as fast as she could.

Since the 1990s, thousands of people have been sharing their ghostly encounters inside Fort Morgan over the Internet. One of these tales was submitted by a man who said he was taking an afternoon stroll with his wife around the fort when they sensed that they were being followed. The couple looked over their shoulders and were surprised to see the emaciated figure of a man in a ragged Confederate uniform. Thinking that someone was playing a joke on them, the man turned around and waved at the soldier. Instead of waving back, the soldier walked over to the seawall and jumped off. After discussing what they had just witnessed, the couple retraced their steps but were unable to find any footsteps other than their own in the sand.

Another contributor reported that his family heard some frightening sounds inside Fort Morgan just before closing time. They had just walked down one of the halls and were entering one of the casements when they heard the sound of a large chain clanking across the floor, as if it was being dragged. At the same time, several of the family members sensed an otherworldly presence inside the room. They conducted a thorough search of the room but found no sign of anything out of the ordinary.

One sighting that has been confirmed by a number of people on the Internet is that of a Confederate soldier standing approximately six feet tall and walking through a wall. In one of these tales, a man took a family photo inside one of the rooms and was surprised to see the image of a man in a Confederate uniform. The soldier's appearance matched the description of the man who has been seen walking through the wall.

A number of paranormal groups have investigated Fort Morgan over the years. One of them, Spirit Seekers Paranormal Investigation, Research, & Intervention Team (S.P.I.R.I.T.) collected some intriguing evidence during their stay at the old fort in 2010. Using the Ghost Radar app on her phone, a female investigator picked up the word "female" in the enlisted men's quarters, an area of the fort where women were not permitted in the nineteenth century. Another response the group received on the Ghost Radar—"Someone doesn't

*Several family members were walking through one of the casements in Fort Morgan when they heard the clanking of a large chain.* (Photo from Wikimedia Commons)

like Europeans"—seems to hearken back to the War of 1812, when many American soldiers harbored negative feelings about the British. S.P.I.R.I.T. also photographed a number of orbs inside the fort. Tony Harrington, a member of the group, admitted that orbs are not accepted as viable evidence by the entire paranormal community. However, he did photograph a light anomaly that seems to have no rational explanation. He took a picture of an area that was roped off for construction, and it clearly shows a strange light hovering six feet off the ground beside the fort. Harrington did not see the light before he took the photograph, and no one was with him at the time. Nor were there any reflective surfaces in the area.

The group's video cameras captured another startling image. Harrington was filming when he saw a shadowy figure approximately four feet tall run down a corridor. The figure appeared to be hunched over. He followed it into a room where several other members of the group were conducting an EVP session. During the session, he distinctly heard footsteps inside the room. No one else heard them, so Harrington asked the spirit to make a sound. This time, the other members heard the noise. The spirit responded to Harrington's request two other times by making a sound that was very clear. Meanwhile, Alan Lowe, the leader of the group, returned to the corridor where Harrington had seen the entity. As he was looking through the viewfinder on his camera, the light dimmed for a few seconds. Lowe surmised that something had cut off the light temporarily by walking between the wall and the viewfinder.

Despite Fort Morgan's growing reputation as a haunted destination, many park officials and historians discount the veracity of the tales. Staff members claim that the fort's apparitions are nothing more than fleeting shadows in sunless rooms and corridors. Tim Johnson, of Living Images, said, "I believe that the history of the fort is what makes the backs of our necks tingle a little." Perhaps Fort Morgan's ghost tales will receive more credence after the paranormal groups that investigate the site on a regular basis produce indisputable proof that the past is not really past.

### Freight House Restaurant
### Hartselle

Hartselle was founded in 1870 but not incorporated until 1875. The town is named after one of the owners of the railroad, George Hartsell. The town's rapid growth coincided with the establishment of a station there for the Louisville and Nashville Railroad in 1872. Logging was the town's primary industry in the early years. At the turn of the century, cotton farming became the residents' main source of income. By 1932, Hartselle had become the center for most of the county's cotton ginning. The town's most notorious episode occurred in 1926 when five men entered the bank with guns drawn. They emptied the safe and took hostages. Four hours later, the thieves escaped with $15,000 in cash and gold. The theft is known as one of the most brazen bank robberies in the history of Alabama.

A fire destroyed twenty-one buildings in 1916, with the exception of the passenger depot (1914) and freight terminal (1915). Both buildings were constructed by the L&N Railroad. Today, the town's biggest draws are the thirty antique and gift shops occupying most of the old buildings in the downtown section and the Freight House Restaurant, which opened in the old freight terminal in 2008.

In the twentieth century, the freight depot served a number of purposes. It was a warehouse for a while for insulation and lumber. In the early 2000s, an antique store operated here. In 2008, Sandra Sowder converted the old building into the Freight House Restaurant. Cotton was loaded through the large semicircular doors in the walls. Most of the doors have been bricked up, but Sandra turned one of them into a fireplace. The booths are paneled with wooden doors taken from old houses.

Karen, a waitress, has seen the spirit haunting the Freight House Restaurant. "If you are at the waitress's station, you will see her out of the corner of your eye," she told me. "One day, my sister-in-law called me—she used to work here too. She wanted me to come in real early. She didn't want to because she was scared. One day, she was the only one here, and all the 'to-go' stuff flew off the shelves. She slept here one night, and the next morning, right in the middle of the walkway was the railroad spike," which is normally on display in the entrance of the restaurant. According to Karen, the kitchen is haunted as well. "One guy was back at the table, and the other guy was working at the grill, when both of them saw something fly across the kitchen right in front of them. They couldn't tell what it was." To Karen's knowledge, the only person who died at the old depot was a man who fell off the loading dock and was hit by a train. However, years ago, the trains deposited caskets containing bodies in the depot and stored them there until the coroner and loved ones had a chance to look at them.

For the most part, Karen has become accustomed to the unearthly presence in the restaurant. "You can feel it every once in a while.

You can hear footsteps. It doesn't bother me. The ghost likes to throw things around. We'll come in in the morning, and we'll find glasses busted on the floor. One or two." Around closing time, though, the restaurant seems to take on a more menacing aura. "When I leave this building at night," Karen said, "you can't get me to look in one of those windows. I don't want one of those things looking back at me."

Sandra Sowder is somewhat skeptical of the building's reported paranormal activity. "Well, you know, I'm in this building in the middle of the night a lot, walking through, in pitch-dark, and nothing's happened to me," she told me. "I have had employees who have had experiences, though, that made their hair stand on end. I've had employees say they've seen blue lights in their peripheral vision. I had one manager who saw an apparition. He said her hair was up, and she had a high-necked-collar dress on. That manager was on vacation on a big holiday we have here: 'Depot Days.' We had a

*Servers at the Freight House Restaurant have heard phantom footsteps and seen blue lights in their peripheral vision.* (Courtesy Marilyn Brown)

guest from New Orleans here, a young lady. She was looking around upstairs, and when she came down, I started talking to her, and she said, 'Do you realize you have spirits here?' I told her that's what I've been told. Then she described the same woman with the swept-up hair and the white dress." Sandra also said that when they open up in the morning, they find cups strewn around. She stated that when the railroad spike appeared on the floor, it was in a spot where the staff would have seen it the night before when they were sweeping up.

## GainesRidge Dinner Club
## Camden

The *I*-frame dwelling in which the GainesRidge Dinner Club is located was built in the late 1820s. It is distinctive not only because of its Federal-style interior and the absence of a center hallway but also because at one time, it was the only two-story building between Blacks Bluff and Allenton. One of the house's first residents was Ebenezer Hearn, a veteran of the War of 1812 and a Methodist minister. He came to Alabama with Andrew Jackson during the Creek Wars. Reverend Hearn established churches from West Alabama to Greensboro and, eventually, to Camden in 1837. Today, he is remembered as the "Father of Methodism" in Alabama.

In 1898, the Gaines family acquired the house. Gen. Edmund Pendleton Gaines (1777-1849) was a veteran of the War of 1812, Seminole Wars, and Black Hawk War. He also captured Aaron Burr at McIntosh Bluffs. Fort Gaines in Mobile Bay is named after him. His brother, George Strother Gaines, was a federal trade agent with the Indian tribes in Alabama and the president of the Mobile Branch Bank. He also negotiated the removal of the Choctaw Indian tribes following the signing of the Treaty of Dancing Rabbit Creek in 1830.

In October 1985, two members of the Gaines family, Betty Kennedy and her sister, Haden G. Marsh, decided to open a restaurant in the family home. "The house in which the dinner club is located has been in my family since 1898," Betty told me. "My great-grandfather, David John Fail, purchased the property from the Hearn estate." The house had stood abandoned for years and was pretty dilapidated. The grounds were overgrown with weeds. "Everybody thought we were crazy," Betty said. "We knew we were not going to name it after my great-grandfather. His name was David John Fail. We were not going to call it 'The Fail Place Inn.' So we settled on 'Gaines' because it was our maiden name, and my father had done a lot of work here, even though he was not a native of Wilcox County. We called it 'GainesRidge.' Most people around here just called it 'The Ridge.'"

Today, people come from miles around to sample the restaurant's black-bottom pie, which was listed online in 100 Dishes to Eat in Alabama Before You Die. The dinner club hosts many types of functions. "We do christening luncheons and family reunions, class reunions. We do ten to twelve wedding receptions a year, sometimes more. We even do funeral luncheons. That's not unusual. So I tell everybody, 'We take care of you from the cradle to the grave.' We can go from a funeral luncheon in the daytime to a cocktail party at night. No one would ever know that one was going on with the other. Not at the same time, of course."

In recent years, the GainesRidge Dinner Club has become as well known for its paranormal activity as for its down-home cooking. Betty Kennedy frequently regales diners with the story of her own ghost encounter. "Now I might embellish a little—a lot. This happened on a night when we were not open, maybe a Monday or a Tuesday. We were getting ready for a luncheon. I was working when I first started the business. I was working for the government. So I had to do things at night because I had to go to work the next day. So I was here one night with one cook named Maggie Bell. She and I were in the kitchen working. It was a still night. It was not a stormy night or a windy night. I needed a cookpot. There are only two rooms upstairs. It's really a small house. We added these two dining rooms. At the time, it was a relatively small building. It's a little enclosed staircase, not a grand stairway, like I wish we had. I went upstairs, turned the light on, and got the pot. And just as I was turning around to come back downstairs, she called me. She just screamed. She said, 'Miss Betty! Miss Betty! Come quick! Oh, Lordy Jesus!' Well, it scared me so bad that I dropped the pot. I hadn't had both knees operated on, so I could move pretty quick. I went flying down those steps—hit about three of them. I turned around and burst into the kitchen, thinking, 'Fire! Blood! Death!' I had no idea what had happened. There she was, calmly chopping onions, but she looked real funny.

"Well, I was so mad. I could have hurt myself," Betty said. "So I said, 'Maggie Bell!' and I used a really bad word. 'What in the hell is the matter?' There she was, just chopping onions. She looked up at me, and she said, 'Miss Betty, it wasn't me that called you.' Now, we were by ourselves. She said she heard the voice too. I said, 'What did it say, Maggie Bell?' She said, 'Come quick, oh Lordy Jesus.' Well, the first thing we did was to look out to see if a car is driving in or if somebody is outside. We looked outside and walked all over the house. So I said, 'Maggie Bell, I left the light upstairs.' She said, 'I ain't going upstairs. I ain't going by myself.' So the two of us crept up the stairs and got up to the top of the steps. We had already searched everywhere. Closets. Bedrooms. Everything. We looked up there and opened the door. The light was off. The pot was on the floor. We looked all through that room and went into the next room. You could walk into that room back then. You can't now because it is full of Christmas decorations and thirty years of whatever. So we went all through that room. We looked everywhere. Nothing. So we turned off the light and went back downstairs. We didn't take the pot because I knew I wasn't going to stay any longer. I said, 'Maggie Bell, can you finish in the morning?' She said, 'Yes ma'am. I'll do whatever you want me to do. Let's just go home and get out of this place, and I'll come back in the daylight.' To this day, I don't know what it was. That's the way it happened to me. To this day, Maggie Bell will tell you that she heard it too. There are two types of stories that old houses in the South have in common. One is the pot of gold that's buried to keep the Yankees from getting. The other is the resident ghost. We have the resident ghost. I'd love to find the pot of gold."

On another occasion, Betty's daughter became a witness to the dinner's club's ghostly activity. "Whenever she's here, something seems to happen," Betty noted. "She came in the kitchen, and she said, 'Mama, you need to come out here. Somebody has fallen in the ladies' restroom.' I could just see lawsuits [being filed]. I was just horrified. I didn't keep cheap rugs or anything in there that you could fall over. So I walked out, and all the waitresses were standing there, looking at the ladies' restroom door. I asked them, 'How do you know there's somebody in there?' They said, 'We heard them fall, and we saw the door shake.' I said, 'Well, open the door.' They said, 'We can't open the door. It's locked.' So I tried, and sure enough, the door wouldn't budge. I said, 'Have you seen anybody come out?' And they said, 'No, we've been standing here, looking at the door.' So I pulled really hard, and the third time, I broke the little latch, which is all we have. So we looked in there, and there was nobody there. No pictures on the floor. No nothing. There was nobody there. Anything out of the way that happens here, we blame it on the ghost."

Betty attributes some of the unearthly occurrences in her establishment to a tragic event that took place there early in the twentieth century. Betty said that a very large woman and her family were renting the house. She had thirteen children, including an infant who slept in bed with her mother one cold winter night. "One night, she rolled over, and she smothered the baby," Betty said. "I'm sure that it was accidental. My mother never told me this story until after we came back here. When we lived here, she never told us about it because she didn't want us to get scared. Some of her family members had told it to her. She wanted to be able to leave us here alone [without us imagining things]. She didn't put up with much foolishness. Probably other people have died here too."

One of the waitresses at the GainesRidge Dinner Club substantiated Betty's insistence that her restaurant is haunted. "I have heard the baby crying, and so have other people," she told me. "They usually hear it in that front room. I can remember one lady who walked up the front step and wouldn't come in here. She said that something bad had happened here, and she wasn't going in. Some people have said that they were driving up to the restaurant, and they saw somebody staring out of the second-story window between the two pillars. I didn't pay much attention to the story until late one evening when I drove up and saw somebody looking down at me from the window. I thought the house was empty, so I searched all over, but I couldn't find anyone there. The scariest thing happened several years ago. I was working behind the counter at the waitress station when I felt something run past my legs. I got a cold feeling as it rushed by. I looked all around, thinking that it was an animal, but nothing was there." One could say that some of the spirits served with the meals are *gratis*.

## Helion Lodge
### Huntsville

The Masons have had a strong presence in Huntsville since Madison Lodge #21 received its charter from the Grand Lodge of Kentucky on August 21, 1811. A second Masonic lodge, Bethesda Lodge #2, was formed in Madison County in 1818. Six years later, the two lodges merged to form Helion Lodge #1. In 1911, the present building was constructed on the site of Madison Lodge #21. Eunomia Masonic Hall, as it was originally known, was designed by a Mason, Edgar Love. It survived the turmoil of the Civil War, despite the Union Army's occupation of thecity. In the first half of the twentieth century, Helion Lodge #1 had the second-largest membership in Alabama, due in large part to the influx of people who moved to Huntsville after World War II. Many of these newcomers were lured by the promise of job openings at the Marshall Space Flight Center and at Redstone Arsenal. Among the lodge's most notable members are Mayor Joe W. Davis and Sen. John Sparkman. In the 1960s, Helion Lodge #1 became the mother lodge of two other lodges: Solar Lodge #914 (1962) and Apollo Lodge #921 (1967). Today, Helion Lodge #1 is the oldest Masonic lodge in Alabama. It is also very haunted.

For years, many residents of Huntsville have suspected that the spirits of former Masons and Grand Masters are still meeting in the old lodge. Several witnesses have seen the apparition of a man on the stairway landing. Passersby have observed lights flickering on and off in different windows late at night. Visitors have captured the image of a large ball of blue light in photographs. One member said that the door to one of the rooms swung open by itself. So many stories of hauntings in Helion Lodge have been circulating around Huntsville that many people are reluctant to even enter the old building.

According to the historian for the lodge, a past master was talking to a friend in front of a wall of portraits of past masters dating back to 1811. While they were discussing one of the paintings, the nameplate jumped off the picture. They thought it was strange but put it back on. As they resumed talking, the entire picture jumped off the wall. "I didn't see it," the historian told me. "I just heard about it. Both of these guys are people who would not make up a story like that." He went on to say that another member, who was in the lodge alone late one night, heard the heavy footsteps of a large person. He tries to keep an open mind about the unexplained occurrences inside the old building. "Sometimes while talking about [the ghostly activity], the hairs will stand up on the back of my neck. If anyone wants to reveal themselves to me, I'll assume that they are a brother. I guess they had such a great time at the lodge that they didn't want to leave."

## Hotel Highland
## Birmingham

The Hotel Highland was originally an eight-story office building called the Medical Arts Building. It was built in 1931 over a period of just six months in the Five Points South area by the Kamram Grotto, a fraternal order of freemasons. The architect, Charles H. McCauley, was inspired by the Art Deco medical towers in Nashville, Chattanooga, St. Louis, and Atlanta. The Birmingham Apothecary and an assortment of shops took up the first floor; doctors' and surgeons' offices were located on the other floors. That same year, the Kamram Grotto converted a garage around the corner into a dance hall called the Pickwick Club, a popular nightspot that burned down in the early 1950s. The Medical Arts Building was in dire need of repairs when a retired cardiac surgeon decided to renovate the old building in the 1980s as a European-style hotel. Named after the former dance club, the Pickwick Hotel closed in 2007 and was transformed once again, this time as a luxurious sixty-three-room boutique hotel called the Hotel Highland.

Since the renovation, ghostly activity has been reported throughout the hotel. Desk clerks at the reservation desk have heard the laughter of a little girl and the bouncing of a ball. Members of the staff assume that this is the same little girl who has been seen playing jacks by the desk. Many times, guests have reported seeing apparitions in their rooms.

Most of the paranormal activity at the Hotel Highland takes place on the eighth floor. While the hotel was being renovated, the most commonly reported ghost on that floor was of a nurse dutifully making her rounds. Staff at the hotel claim that occasionally, the elevator rises up to the eighth floor on its own. One night, a guest sleeping in her room on that floor was awakened by a harsh male voice telling her to get out. Two female specters have been seen in the hallway on the fourth floor. A "friendly" female spirit roams the halls of the fifth floor.

Guests exercising in the gym area in the basement have had strange experiences as well. Some people have felt an uncomfortable presence during their workout. A few guests have experienced a sudden drop in temperature in specific parts of the gym. Others have smelled the sweet fragrance of flowers. Breezes coming out of nowhere waft through the basement occasionally. The reason for the large number of weird incidents may be found in the building's past. For decades, the basement served as the morgue for the hospital.

## The Huntsville Railroad Depot
### Huntsville

Built in 1860, the Huntsville Depot is the oldest existing railroad depot in Alabama. It served as the Eastern Division Headquarters for the Memphis and Charleston Railroad. It had the first indoor plumbing in Huntsville. On April 11, 1862, Union general Ormsby McKnight Mitchel captured the Huntsville Depot, severing an essential Confederate east-west railroad link. His troops commandeered a train on its way from the Shiloh battlefield and captured 159 Confederate soldiers. The soldiers were held on the third floor of the depot for ten days before being sent to Union prison camps. For the rest of the war, the depot and Huntsville itself were in the hands of the Union Army. The depot was used to funnel Union supplies to the Western Theater. After the Civil War, the Union Army returned control of the depot and railroad to the city. However, because the Federal soldiers had torn up miles of track, the Memphis and Charleston Railroad never got out of receivership and was forced to declare bankruptcy. In 1898, the Southern Railway took over operations, and the depot became part of their division headquarters. The Huntsville Depot was part of Teddy Roosevelt's "Whistle Stop Campaign" through twenty-three states. In 1912, it was renovated. The wood planks on the first level were replaced with a concrete floor. The stairs between the first and second levels were moved to give the superintendents' offices, accounting office, and paymaster's office more privacy. The banisters were cut in pieces and removed. Troops were moved out of Huntsville through the depot during the Spanish-American War, World War I, and World War II. In 1950, Dr. Wernher von Braun and his team of scientists passed through the Huntsville Depot. It continued to serve the city until 1968. After the Huntsville Depot was placed on the National Register of Historic Places, a campaign was initiated to prevent it from being demolished. In the early 1980s, the depot became part of the Early Works Museum.

Today, the second and third floors are unaltered. On the first level, an elevator and drinking fountain were installed, and the stairway and banisters were rebuilt. During the restoration process, the handwritten names of Confederate soldiers and of railroad workers dating back to the 1890s were discovered on the walls of the

*In 1862, the Union Army turned the Huntsville Depot into a prison camp for Confederate soldiers.* (Photo from Wikimedia Commons)

*The penciled names of Confederate prisoners still adorn sections of the walls on the third floor.* (Courtesy Marilyn Brown)

upper floors. Unfortunately, years of exposure to sunlight have caused some the penciled signatures to fade. Experts in the paranormal believe that the changes made in the building may have awakened some of the depot's dormant spirits.

Jim, one of the depot's tour guides, told me that sometimes, he hears noises when the building is empty. "You turn off the lights, and you hear faint voices. If there are two people in here who hear the same sound at the same time, that's pretty convincing proof. The paranormal groups that have investigated the depot have detected some weird energy levels here, but that's about it. So we tell people there's a possibility that the depot's haunted."

In her book *Haunted North Alabama*, Jessica Penot recounts some of the paranormal experiences visitors have had in the Huntsville Depot. People have seen a face staring down at them from a second-story window. The apparition of a former railroad engineer has been sighted on the tracks. On the third floor, visitors have encountered strange flickering lights. Undoubtedly, people interested in proving the existence of the paranormal account for a large percentage of the visitors to the Huntsville Depot each year.

### The Josephine Hotel
### Union Springs

On August 25, 1879, Dr. Robert A. Fleming began making plans to build a luxury hotel on property occupied by two frame buildings owned by N. B. Powell and Hanson & Son. When the Josephine Hotel was completed in August 1880, the *Union Springs Herald* hailed it as a "thing of beauty." The writer said that Fleming erected the hotel as a tribute to his wife, Josephine. The writer went on to describe its most prominent features: "The building is three stories in height and is furnished with the modern conveniences of an elevator and waterworks, the water supply being obtained from a water supply in the rear of the hotel. The outside appearance of the Josephine is pleasing and is an ornament to Prairie Street almost equal to our magnificent courthouse; but the visitor on entering will be more impressed by the beauty and convenience of the interior. The rooms are commodious, and the peculiarities of our Southern climate are met by the ventilation that is secured from lofty ceilings and transoms. For the convenience of regular boarders, several suites of rooms have been arranged that will compare favorably with those of metropolitan hotels. The interior is tastefully finished with trimmings of walnut and heart pine."

In the early years, mercantile shops occupied the first floor of the 17,000-square-foot building. Two double-door entrances separated the three main areas on the first floor. The hotel had a total of thirty-two rooms on the second and third floors. The large hallways on the second and third floors were illuminated by skylights. Some of the Josephine Hotel's guests were merchants who came to town to peddle their goods. Many of the region's most influential politicians frequented the saloon on the first floor, primarily because of the high quality of its whiskey. The Josephine also served the finest food in town, including wild ducks, geese, quail, and pigeons brought to the hotel by local hunters.

As the ownership of the hotel changed, so did the name. A druggist named F. F. Ravencroft purchased the building in 1903 and set up his pharmacy inside the hotel. After completely renovating the hotel, Ravencroft made W. T. Hough the business manager; Miss Kate Brown was put in charge of housekeeping. On April 11, 1917, C. E. Gholston purchased the hotel from W. A. and Annie Robertson and changed the name to the Drummers Hotel. On January 18, 1923, a Mrs. Cook bought the property and renamed it the Commercial Hotel. Over the years, a number of different businesses have occupied a section of the hotel, including Jinks Saloon, an oyster bar, tire store, suede clothing store, and hair salon.

Joyce Perrin is the current owner of the Josephine Hotel. For her, restoring the building has been a labor of love. Today, the first floor consists of a café area and a display of local arts and crafts called the Josephine Arts Center. "We use the bottom floor to make enough money to fix the other floors," Perrin told me. The hotel's past has proven to be a reliable source of income. Ghost tours, led by author Faith Serafin, have made the Josephine a popular destination for lovers of all things paranormal. "We decided to do the ghost thing because we looked on the Internet and saw the money that could be made from bringing people in," Perrin said. "Old people come to Union Springs to look at the houses; young people come to look for ghosts. Faith brings around two dozen people here each time on tours, and she brings just about that many people to help her. They break them up into three groups. One group comes up here, the second group goes to the jail, and the third group goes to the cemetery. Faith and her people conduct the tours, and all I do is get a percentage." Perrin added that the ghost tours have become even more popular since the Josephine Hotel's appearance on the television series *Ghost Asylum*.

The paranormal activity in the hotel takes many forms, according to Joyce Perrin. "We've had ghosts talk to people. People on the tours have sworn that they have heard the piano play. Sometimes, people smell pipe and cigar smoke in the saloon area. The ghost of Josephine has been seen from the windows of the hotel. One night, when we first started our overnight events, one of the pictures flew off the wall on the bottom floor." Fittingly, an old sheet of piano music found on the second floor is a song about a ghost.

Historical research is an integral part of the tours and investigations held at the Josephine Hotel. On one investigation, a ghost gave his name. "The group went upstairs one night and came back down," Perrin said. "They said that some entity had made itself known on the back staircase. Somebody asked him his name, and he said, 'Jefferson.'" Perrin added that five ghosts have revealed their identity since the tours started at the Josephine Hotel, but Jefferson was the easiest to identify. "Joseph Burfour has close connections to the Cowan family. He was either Josephine's brother-in-law or the kin of Josephine's brother-in-law. He fought in the Civil War," Perrin said.

Perrin admits that the hotel can be a scary place at times, especially when she is by herself, but most of the disturbances have a logical explanation. "I used to stay here a lot with my dog, and there were all kinds of noises up there at night, but a lot of it was plaster falling because of the rain. We fixed the roof, so we can't blame the noises on falling plaster anymore. Some nights, I have brought my dog up here with me, and he runs home, for some reason. We've never had aggressive ghosts, though. Most people who come here say it's a very friendly place."

## Lucas Tavern
## Montgomery

Lucas Tavern is a four-room inn with a long central hall. It consists of a kitchen, dining room, main tavern room, and bedroom. It was originally built on the Federal Road just west of Line Creek. James Abercrombie became the first proprietor of the inn in 1818. Three years later, Walter B. Lucas purchased it. Under his ownership, Lucas Tavern became a popular overnight stop for weary travelers. Guests dined on chicken, ham, vegetables, sweet pies, preserved fruit, pudding and sauce, and a dessert consisting of strawberries and plums soaked in wine and brandy. The Marquis de Lafayette was a guest at the inn on April 2, 1825, while touring the United States. Lucas Tavern became a private residence in the 1840s. A number of different families occupied the home for approximately a hundred years. By the 1960s, the building was abandoned and in dire need of repair. The Landmarks Foundation bought the former inn in 1978 and moved it to 310 North Hull Street in Old Alabama Town. Lucas Tavern was fully restored in 1980.

Stories of paranormal activity in Lucas Tavern surfaced in the early 1980s, suggesting that the restoration had awakened one of the inn's dormant spirits. The apparition of a five-foot three-inch woman in her twenties, wearing a Victorian-era dress, is said to have appeared to a number of guests. She is usually seen standing in the doorway or a window, waving and smiling at people walking down the street. In 1985, a man entered the tavern and asked the tour guide if he could meet the young woman who had greeted him in the doorway. She is thought to be the spirit of Eliza Lucas, the daughter of Walter B. Lucas, who served as the hostess of the inn for many years. This normally cordial specter displayed her angry side late one afternoon during a committee meeting that was being held in front of the fireplace. One committee member lost his temper and began shaking his fist and shouting. Suddenly, a cloud of soot belched from the fireplace, covering the irate man with ashes. Eliza's temper flared once again when two staff members were sitting in the tavern, criticizing the way Old Alabama Town was being operated. Without warning, the door to the room crashed to the floor.

The ghost stories of Lucas Tavern have been published in books and recounted on the Internet for many years. During the summer of 2016, this writer asked the current director about the haunting of the inn. She discussed the matter with the tour guides and discovered that the stories were fabricated back in the 1990s by a former employee who was trying to generate interest in Old Town. The fact that no new tales have surfaced in recent years suggests that the stories of the ghost of Eliza Lucas might indeed be apocryphal.

### The Lyric Theatre
### Birmingham

Construction of the Lyric Theatre began in 1912 on three adjoining lots purchased by real-estate developer Louis V. Clark. The Hendon Hetrack Construction Company built the six-story theater and office building at 1800 Third Avenue North, on the corner of Eighteenth Street North. It was Birmingham's first building to be constructed of steel and concrete. The theater took up the first floor, and business offices were housed on the floors above. Clark partnered with Jake Wells to operate the theater. When the Lyric opened on January 14, 1914, as a vaudeville theater, it had 1,583 seats on the main floor as well as two opera boxes and two balconies. A water tank was installed under a center section of the floor for aquatic shows and air conditioning. During the hot summer months, fans were used to blow cool air from as much as two tons of ice deposited in the water tank as a rudimentary form of air conditioning. Until 1926, B. F. Keith Shows booked all of the vaudeville acts at the Lyric Theatre. In the beginning, seven different acts performed each week, with three nightly performances and Saturday matinees. A number of famous entertainers appeared there, including Mae West, the Marx Brothers, Gene Autry, Milton Berle, Eddie Cantor, Sophie Tucker, Fred Allen, and Jack Benny. Admission was between twenty-five and seventy-five cents. For over ten years, the Lyric was known as the city's premier vaudeville theater. Until the 1930s, the Independent Presbyterian Church held Sunday-evening services there.

Like most theaters in the South in the first half of the twentieth century, the Lyric Theatre was segregated. White theatergoers entered through the doors on Third Avenue; African-Americans had to enter from Eighteenth Street, climb a flight of stairs, walk down a long hallway, climb up another stairway to the landing, and then walk up four steps to the "colored balcony." However, the Lyric Theatre was progressive in the sense that it was one of the first theaters in the South that permitted blacks and whites to pay the same price for tickets and to watch performances and movies at the same time.

The decline of the Lyric Theatre began in the 1920s when a number of other theaters opened in Birmingham, including the Masonic Temple Theatre and the Empire Theatre. Business really began to drop off in 1926 after the opening of the first fully air conditioned theater in Birmingham—the Ritz. Business suffered even more during the Great Depression. Following the suicide of Jake Wells in 1927, the mortgage company assumed ownership of the Lyric Theatre and leased it to the Schubert organization. Vaudeville acts continued performing there, but by the end of the 1920s, that form of entertainment had become passé. The increasing popularity of movies and radio led to the closure of the Lyric Theatre in 1931.

In 1932, brothers Ben and L. A. Stein converted it into a movie theater. Renovations included the installment of a new Western

Electric sound system. Four feature films were shown each week. By the end of the year, the Lyric had become a second-run theater. It was renovated once again in the early 1940s, with new projectors. Ervin Jackson & Associates bought the theater out of foreclosure in 1945; five years later, the Acme Theaters chain purchased the Lyric. To make room for the fifteen-by-thirty-six-foot screen for Cinemascope films, the new owners removed the opera boxes in 1954. For a short while, the "Saturday Night Jamboree," held weekly at eleven o'clock, brought back live performances to the Lyric Theatre.

In 1958, the Lyric Theatre closed once again, although the adjoining office building remained open. The theater reopened in 1972, this time as the Grand Bijou. It was a "niche" theater that specialized in showing classic films, such as *The Jazz Singer* with Al Jolson. A short while later, the theater reopened as the Foxy Adult Cinema. The name would change once again to the Roxy Adult Cinema. The Lyric closed in 1980. A nonprofit organization called Birmingham Landmarks acquired the building from the Waters family in 1993.

Restoring the Lyric Theatre to its former glory was a daunting project. Because of the absence of climate control, the interior of the Lyric Theatre had deteriorated badly over the years. Much of the paint in the lobby had faded and was peeling off the walls. A forklift was parked in one of the corners. Garbage was everywhere. However, the mural above the stage, the intricate carvings on the walls, and the asbestos curtains were fairly well preserved.

After a failed attempt to raise funds to restore the old theater in 1998, plans to renovate the building were revived in 2009 with a grant of $200,000 from the city of Birmingham to conduct a feasibility study, which estimated that the Lyric Theatre could bring in $3.5 million annually. In March 2013, a fundraising campaign, "Light Up the Lyric," was launched. By 2014, $7.4 million had been raised to restore the interior of the building.

After an $11 million renovation, the historic theater finally reopened on January 14, 2016. The lineup included the Birmingham Sunlights, Sharif Simmons, Dolores Hydock, and a troupe from the Red Mountain Theatre Company. More than a century after its first performances, the Lyric Theatre was, once again, one of Birmingham's architectural gems.

Over the years, the Lyric Theatre acquired a reputation of being haunted. Most of the paranormal activity reported there includes noises, voices, cold spots, and even full-body apparitions. Several paranormal investigations have been conducted at the Lyric Theatre. In 2009, Tuscaloosa Paranormal Research Group spent the night inside. The members noted several spikes on their EMF meters, but all of this evidence had rational explanations. During the last hour of the investigation, the group collected eight EVPs in the office room on the second floor. In 2011, another group spent a night walking through the office rooms, dressing rooms, and stage. Several members had some startling experiences inside the theater. An unseen hand touched the shoulder of one member on the fourth floor. Everyone in the group heard the disembodied footsteps of someone walking up and down the stairs from the first-floor theater area to the first

*The paranormal activity in the Lyric Theatre includes ghostly voices, cold spots, and full-body apparitions. The completely restored theater reopened on January 14, 2016.* (Photo from Wikimedia Commons)

balcony. Their EMF meter registered several hits as well. Before leaving, the members played a CD of vaudeville music on the stage. Their videorecorders captured strange noises in the theater—clicks and bumps—that were not audible when the CD was being played.

Brant Beene, the director of the Lyric Theatre, told me that a photographer may have inadvertently collected some intriguing evidence of the paranormal. "When we were finishing the plasterwork in the theater, a guy named Joe De Sciose was asked to take a photograph of one of the walls in the 'colored entrance' hallway. He did, and when he got the print back and started looking at it, it showed multiple faces in the plaster as it was drying. We don't have any stories of people dying or ghosts walking the halls or anything, but that image is very startling."

## Old Covington County Jail
### Andalusia

The Old Covington County Jail in Andalusia was in use between 1900 and 1970. One year after it was built, the jail was the focus of one of the only cases of martial law in the state of Alabama. On December 6, 1901, Sheriff Bradshaw and Gov. William D. Jelks alerted the National Guard that 400 men were likely to start a riot outside of the Covington County Jail. At the time, twenty-five black men who had been accused of killing a U.S. marshal and a merchant in Opp were being housed inside. Before finally being stopped in their tracks on their way to the jail, the angry mob managed to kill three black men in Opp and burn another man alive.

One of the many killers who later found themselves incarcerated inside the Covington County Jail was Reuben Alford, who murdered a forest ranger named Will Turbeville on September 1, 1934. His confession led to the release of forest ranger W. E. Jordan and two other men, all of whom were already doing time for Turbeville's murder. Two other men were also arrested and charged with the killing.

The jail's most famous inmate was Hank Williams. The story

goes that he was arrested for leaving his son, Hank Williams, Jr., in a car while he performed at a club in Andalusia. Someone who saw the child alone inside the car notified the police, who arrested Hank on a "drunk and disorderly" charge. His son was placed in child protective services for the night, and Hank was placed in the Old Covington County Jail.

The Old Covington County Jail was closed in 1970 and replaced by a newer structure. In 1989, it was added to the National Register of Historic Places. Over the years, the huge steel-and-concrete building's ominous appearance as well as the rumors of mistreatment of inmates have led many locals to believe that spirits must be sitting

*The spirit of Hank Williams may be one of the ghosts that haunts the Old Covington County Jail.* (Courtesy Amanda Nolin)

in the abandoned cells, waiting for the release that never comes.

In 2009, a local police officer, Roger Cender, and local historical society member, Sue Bass, invited the Alabama Paranormal Research Team (A.P.R.T.) to investigate the old jail. Six team members spent two nights there monitoring the paranormal activity with thermal readers, night-surveillance equipment, EMF detectors, and digital cameras. Faith Serafin, the cofounder of A.P.R.T., immediately got the impression that there was something "odd" about the jail, even before she entered the building. The solitary-confinement cell on the second floor also gave her a "creepy" feeling. Her suspicions that the jail might be haunted were confirmed by the high amount of paranormal activity in places such as the boiler room. The members recorded some very unsettling EVPs in one particular location. "Roger and I were standing inside of the general-population area, popping a set of handcuffs," Serafin said. "We asked out loud, 'Are you upset that a police officer is in the room?' Well, we didn't hear anything then, but on the audio, it said, 'Yep.' It was definitely a man's voice."

After the second night, Serafin left the Old Covington County Jail convinced that they had been inside a haunted location. "That place is haunted beyond a shadow of a doubt," she said. "There's too much evidence, and it's haunted by more than a few ghosts."

## The Pauly Jail
## Union Springs

Most paranormal groups place abandoned prisons at the top of their list of locations likely to be haunted. One of these hotspots in Alabama is the Pauly Jail in Union Springs, which replaced the jail on West Hardaway Street. This boxlike, three-story brick structure was built in 1897 on the Pull House blacksmith lot by the Pauly Jail Building Company, which specialized in steel jail construction. The interior, including the door, dining table and benches, stairs, and lattice in the small cells, was made entirely of metal, with the exception of the wooden windows and attic vent above the door. Frank Anderson was awarded the contract for the sheet-metal work. The exterior includes a number of distinctive architectural features, such as the metal hipped roof and turrets with spiked metal caps called "witch's hats." The supervisor of construction, J. A. Youngblood, built the jail at a cost of $7,250.

The cold, metallic furnishings did little to diminish the jail's oppressive atmosphere. A catwalk surrounding the jail area enabled guards to keep the prisoners under constant surveillance. In the early 1900s, a trapdoor was set in the floor of the third level for the purpose of hanging prisoners. It was released by pulling a lever. Despite the jail's formidable, castle-like appearance, the most determined prisoners could not be prevented from escaping.

In 2004, the jail's austere appearance made it the perfect setting for the film *Heavens Fall*. Produced by the Strata Production Company, it told the story of the trial of the Scottsboro Boys, nine black youths who were falsely accused of raping two white women. The cast included Timothy Hutton, Leelee Sobieski, Anthony Mackie, and Azura Skye.

The Pauly Jail is one of last nineteenth-century jails still standing in Alabama. According to Joyce Perrin, it also harbors a number of angry spirits. "The gallows is still there, and there's a story that at least one person was hanged there. A lot of bad people stayed there and died there. The jail was not air conditioned in the summer or heated in the winter, so life there was pretty hard for the prisoners." Not surprisingly, a large number of the EVPs that have been recorded inside are profane.

The former sheriff of Bullock County had a painful encounter with one of these malicious spirits when he and several other ghost hunters spent a night in the old jail. "The night he was there, one of the ghosts started talking about a politician who died under mysterious circumstances," Perrin said. "The sheriff was trying to antagonize the ghost, and he got hit on the back of the head. He didn't think much about it when it happened, but when he came over to the Josephine Hotel, he said, 'My neck's been bothering me.'

*Built in 1897, the Pauly Jail is one of the last nineteenth-century jails still standing in Alabama.* (Courtesy Marilyn Brown)

So we pulled back his collar, and he had a red spot about the size of a dime on his neck. It had a point on it, and there was blood under the skin. I am a nurse, so while the rest of the group was debriefing, I decided to take another look at it, but he was gone."

The ghosts of the Pauly Jail make their presence known in other ways as well. Visitors have reported hearing disembodied footsteps as well bumping and banging sounds. Shadowy figures and cold spots are encountered on a fairly regular basis. Some of the people incarcerated at the Pauly Jail years ago seem to have been given an extended sentence.

## Pickens County Courthouse
## Carrollton

In the book *13 Alabama Ghosts and Jeffrey*, Kathryn Tucker Windham presents her version of this tale. It begins on April 5, 1865, when Gen. John Croxton's troops burned down the Pickens County Courthouse. After the war, the citizens of Carrollton rebuilt it, but it was burned down again.

Understandably, the citizens of Pickens County were outraged, because the building had come to represent the restoration of their pride and dignity. The sheriff was under a great deal of pressure to apprehend the culprit, so he pinned the crime on a mean-spirited black man named Henry Wells, who had a criminal record. While the courthouse was being rebuilt, Henry learned that he was the sheriff's prime suspect, so he left town in a hurry. Two years later, Henry received word that his grandmother was gravely ill, so he returned to Carrollton under the cover of darkness. As Henry was walking up to the house, the sheriff emerged from the shadows and grabbed him by the arm. Henry was taken into custody and held in the garret of the Pickens County Courthouse on February 8, 1878. As the sun dipped below the horizon, he looked out the window at a large crowd forming on the courthouse lawn. As lightning flashed across the sky, Henry exclaimed, "I am an innocent man. If you hang me, I will be with you always!" Of course, the mob could not hear him, so two of the men flung open the doors of the courthouse and dragged Henry down the stairs. One member of the crowd produced a rope, and within a matter of minutes, Henry Wells was lynched from a tree in front of the courthouse. The next day, two members of the lynch mob were walking past the courthouse when they noticed a face staring down at them from the garret window. They raced up the stairs and were surprised to find the garret empty. Over the next few days, hundreds of people congregated outside of the courthouse to catch a glimpse of the spectral face. The guilt-ridden sheriff carried buckets of water up the steps day after day in a futile attempt to remove the image from the glass. Ironically, his efforts only made the face more distinct. Windham adds that in 1920, a hailstorm broke every window in the courthouse except for the lower right-hand pane of the garret window.

In interviews collected by the WPA in the 1930s, the central figure is Burkhalter, Wells' partner in crime. An interview with an unknown informant contained many of the elements of Windham's story but changed Wells' name and the location of the lynching:

> The Negro Burkhalter was being taken to the state prison of Montgomery after being convicted of burning the courthouse of Pickens County. A group of Carrolton citizens, so the story goes, took Burkhalter away from the posse and hanged him from a huge tree in a swamp during a terrific thunderstorm. Before he was killed, the mob asked the victim if he wanted to make a statement. "I am innocent," he said, "and you will always have my face to haunt you." Undeterred by the protestation of innocence, he was swung up, and as the rope tightened, there was a blinding flash of lightning. Next morning, back home in Carrollton, one of the mob passed the courthouse and saw Burkhalter's likeness on a pane of glass in one of the windows. An investigation from the inside showed the pane perfectly clear. However, in certain lights, many saw the likeness of the Negro from the outside. The glass remained in place, even during a severe hailstorm.

In 1993 Lin Estes told me that, according to the story she heard, a black man was hanged because he raped a white woman, even though he denied having done it. After the hanging, his face appeared on the courthouse window. When the window was replaced following a fire, the face reappeared. Cleaning women tried to remove the face with steel wool and turpentine but to no avail.

In another interview I recorded in 1993, a former gandy dancer named Charlie Vinson said that a brick courthouse replaced the original wooden one. After the face appeared, the window was boarded up. Eventually, a new window was installed, but the face returned. The man who told Charlie the story swore that it was true.

Carrollton resident Robert Hugh Kirksey, who served as probate judge from 1962 to 1981, is very familiar with the legend of Henry Wells. In fact, he was asked to write the text of the historical marker that stands in front of the Pickens County Courthouse. The version of the tale that Kirksey puts the most stock in was recounted in the memoirs of a bounty hunter named John L. Hunnicut, who practiced his profession in Pickens County during Reconstruction. "He was a rounder, and he liked to tell big stories about how tough he was," Kirksey informed me. "One of the stories he told had to do with the capture of the black man Henry Wells, who was reputed to have burned the courthouse in 1876. Of course, it had been burned earlier by Croxton's troops. The day after they burned the University of Alabama, Croxton sent his troops over here to see what was coming out of Mississippi at that time. They came to Carrollton to burn down a commissary that contained supplies, and they burned down the courthouse too. After the Civil War, they rebuilt the courthouse as a frame building. In 1876, Henry Wells and another black man named Burkhalter went on a burglary. I don't think this is entirely a legend. There is some truth in it. They got in the courthouse to see if they could find some money. One of the stories was that Wells had been indicted for some crimes. Wells believed that if the indictment was burned, they couldn't try him. This is just a legend. I think it is more likely that they attempted to cover up the robbery by burning down the courthouse. In his book, Hunnicut claims that he found Wells in Tuscaloosa County hiding out and brought him back to

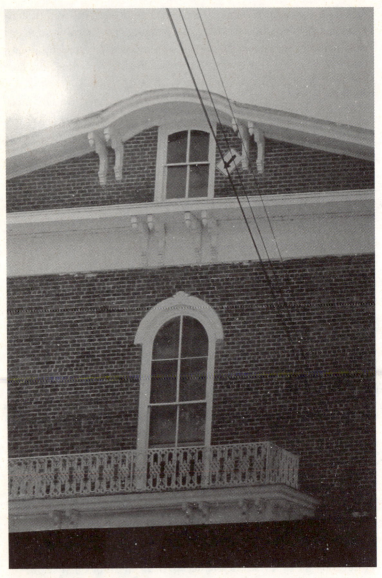

*The face of Henry Wells still stares down from the garret window of the Pickens County Courthouse.* (Courtesy Marilyn Brown)

Carrollton. Basically, the story I heard is that Henry was placed in the attic for safekeeping from a mob and lightning struck and illuminated his face as he peered down at them and said, 'If you hang me, I will be with you always.' And after they hanged him, his face appeared on the garret window the next day and is still there."

The social significance of the legend of Henry Wells came to the forefront during the civil rights movement. "I remember back in the 1960s before the integration of the public schools took place, a teacher called me from Birmingham and said she had a fifth-grade class that wanted to see the face in the window," Kirksey said. "They were doing a project on folklore, and she wondered if I would tell them about the face in the window. I said, 'Sure.' The day for their visit arrived, and I was standing outside of the courthouse. Two Trailways buses pulled up. The children came out of the bus, and they were all black. I remember thinking that I had never told the story to black people before. I had always told it to people from the culture that I came out of. Well, I decided that I would just tell them the truth. So I got them in the auditorium right across the street, and I told them the story. I tried to think about what I could say to let them know that I saw this incident as a bad thing, and I wound up saying something like, 'You might ask what the face in the courthouse window is saying. It says to me, "Don't ever let this happen again!"'"

## Rawls Hotel
### Enterprise

The Rawls Hotel was built in 1903 by Capt. Japheth Rawls, who established one of the first turpentine plants in Coffee County. He and his wife, Elizabeth, modeled their two-story, stucco-faced hotel after a hotel they had seen while visiting Florida. Rawls spared no expense on his hotel, using teakwood for the doors, cherry wood for the stairway, and chestnut for the fluted pillars. Following Rawls' death in 1925, the hotel was passed down to his nephew Jesse P.

Rawls' wife, Margaret. The couple immediately planned to transform it into the sort of hostelry that would attract travelers arriving in the train depot. In 1928, two three-story wings were added to the hotel. They also installed elegant chandeliers in the lobby, which was lined with decorative columns. The Rawls Hotel soon gained fame as the first building in Enterprise with heated grates and electric lights. Not coincidentally, Jesse Rawls was the founder of Enterprise's electrical power system. Nowadays, the historic Rawls Hotel is as famous for its ghosts as it is for its grand ballroom, fine restaurant, and well-stocked wine cellar.

Overnight guests have been reporting paranormal activity in the hotel for decades. Several years ago, a psychic guest sensed the presence of spirits the moment she walked through the door. Full-body apparitions have been sighted on the second and third floors. The spectral giggling of children resounds throughout the third story and outside of the restaurant. An employee claimed to have seen the apparition of a twelve-year-old girl running down a hallway. People have heard doors open and close in empty rooms at all hours. The unmistakable odor of cigars and perfume wafts through deserted hallways and vacant rooms. In the 1990s, a male guest told the desk clerk that during the night, he had heard vintage television shows, such as *Mr. Ed* and *Captain Kangaroo,* coming from rooms on the second and third floors, even though these shows had not been on the air for many years. Kitchen workers have placed a stirring spoon or spatula in one place and found that it had been moved somewhere else after they turned around. Another employee heard piano music playing in the ballroom late one night. When she opened the door, she was surprised to find no one there.

The dominant spirit in the hotel is assumed to be the ghost of Japheth Rawls. One employee saw his apparition, dressed in overalls, working on the pipes in the cellar. One day, an employee named Hayden Pursley was assigned the task of hanging draperies in the ballroom. The process was made even more tedious by the fact that for two days, after hanging up the draperies, he would find them down the next morning. Finally, on the third day, the invisible

*Capt. Japheth Rawls is one of several spirits haunting the Rawls Hotel.* (Photo from Wikimedia Commons)

culprit expressed its disapproval of the window treatments by hurling a board across the room and hitting Pursley in the head. Apparently, Japheth is still overseeing the daily operations of the hotel.

In October 2002, *Southeast Sun* staff writer Carole Brand decided to test the validity of the tales of the Rawls Hotel's ghostly activity that had been circulating around Enterprise since the end of World War I. While she was touring the wine cellar with a group of hotel workers at 10:02 P.M., her friend said that she observed three children dressed in the fashions of the 1920s. At that same moment, Brand's thermometer indicated that the temperature was thirty-five degrees, making it much colder in this corner of the basement than in the rest of the hotel. She also observed a man wearing a mustache and grey overalls.

At 12:21 A.M., Brand was walking from the ballroom to the kitchen when she discovered that the swing door would not open. "The group behind me laughed, thinking I was doing it on purpose, but I know I wasn't." At that moment, Brand found it difficult to breathe. She reached in her bag for her Polaroid camera and temperature gauge. Brand was surprised to find that they were missing, even though she had seen them there a few minutes before. When she turned around, she noticed an employee with her hand on her chest. She too had felt suffocated in the room. Twenty minutes later, they were still totally exhausted. They felt as if something had completely drained them of energy. Brand gazed down and found her temperature gauge sitting on top of her bag, and her Polaroid was underneath it. She snapped a few shots, but nothing showed up on the pictures. As Brand leaving the hotel, her attention was drawn to a window in the grand ballroom. A young woman, dressed in white, was looking down at her. Within a few seconds, she was gone.

My wife, Marilyn, and I stayed at the Rawls Hotel in 2006. We spent the night in one of the most haunted rooms. We took multiple photographs with our digital cameras but were unable to catch anything remotely paranormal. We also held an EVP session but did not record any unusual sounds. However, when I was sitting on the edge of the bed, holding my EMF meter, the gauge spiked all the way to red for about ten seconds. No electrical appliances were anywhere near the meter. Although we collected no empirical evidence of a haunting inside the room, I like to think that one of the spirits dropped in to say hello before we went to sleep.

## St. James Hotel
### Selma

Built in 1837, the St. James is one of the longest-running hotels in Alabama. For years, it was known as the Brantley Hotel. The outer rooms offered guests a grand view of the Alabama River; from the inner rooms, guests could see the courtyard and fountain. Businessmen, planters, soldiers, and a few disreputable individuals made the hotel their "home away from home." A new owner gave the hotel a new name—the Troupe House—and his slave, Benjamin S. Turner, became the manager. Turner went on to become the first African-American mayor of Selma and the first African-American

U.S. congressman. The hotel survived the Battle of Selma, largely because it served as the temporary barracks for the Union Army. Except for a few other buildings on Water Avenue, most of the city was destroyed. The primary targets of the Union Army were the Confederate arsenals and batteries. In 1871, Capt. Tom Smith bought the hotel and named it the St. James Hotel. The most notorious guests were Frank and Jesse James, who stayed there while visiting Selma on holiday in 1881. At that time, the hotel operated more as an apartment house where guests could rent rooms for an extended period of time. The hotel closed in 1892, just before the Panic of 1893. Over the next few decades, the building was used for a variety of purposes, including a tire recapping business, storage and office space, and a feed store. A few drastic changes were made in the building as well. Several wings were razed, and the first floor was gutted. Hopes of restoring the hotel to its former glory were revived in the 1990s, when the community of Selma and a group of investigators initiated a $6 million restoration project. The work was completed in 1997, and the hotel reopened. Visitors to Selma are attracted by the hotel's nineteenth-century splendor. They also stay there in the hope of meeting the ghosts of the St. James' most famous guests.

Psychics have detected the presence of three spirits inside the hotel. A number of guests on the second floor have had their sleep interrupted by the incessant barking of a dog. When the night clerk searches the floors for the obnoxious canine, no dog is ever found. Some guests have also heard the clicking of a dog's nails as it runs down the halls at night. It is important to note that the St. James is a "no-pets-allowed" hotel.

John Jewett, the general manager of the hotel, believes that the dog belongs to the ghost of Jesse James. For years, people have seen a rugged-looking cowboy in nineteenth-century attire wearing a gun belt. He is usually sighted coming out of Rooms 214, 314, or 315. People are alerted to James' presence by the jingling of his spurs. Jesse's ghost has also been seen sitting at his favorite table, which is to the left of the bar.

*Some say the ghost of Jesse James is still a guest at the St. James Hotel.* (Photo from Wikimedia Commons)

The third ghost is the spirit of the girlfriend of Jesse James, Lucinda. Eyewitnesses describe her as a tall, attractive, dark-haired apparition. She is usually seen walking around the hotel at night. "She's going about her business," Jewett said. "Guests are made aware of her presence by the distinctive scent of lavender. We've had some people come down very shaken because they think she talks to them. For the most part, people say she merely looks at them." A few visitors claim to have seen Lucinda floating through the bar area. Some people believe that she is the figure in the "ghost photograph" on display at the front desk.

The poltergeist activity that occurs on a regular basis at the hotel cannot be attributed to any specific entity. A cook staying in Room 304 was awakened by a flashing light. She also said that the curtains were moving on their own. In the kitchen, dishes have rattled, shattered, or disappeared, and eyewitnesses have seen lights flicker and doors shut by themselves. Cold spots appear in different parts of the kitchen. People passing through the kitchen have been touched by invisible fingers. A psychic walking into the room claims to have made contact with the spirit of a former occupant who cannot "pass over to the other side" because he has unfinished business to tend to.

Paranormal investigators have gathered some intriguing evidence from the St. James Hotel. During an EVP session in the bar area, an investigator asked, "Is anyone here?" When the recording was replayed, the investigators heard a clear voice saying, "That's a stupid question." That same night, the investigators captured images of people in nineteenth-century clothing sitting in the courtyard.

The St. James has forty-two rooms, each lovingly restored to its nineteenth-century appearance. Although all of the rooms are attractive, the most appealing for ghost hunters are the ones where the resident ghosts refuse to check out.

## Sloss Furnaces
## Birmingham

James Withers Sloss was born in Mooresville, Alabama, on April 7, 1820. He got his start as an apprentice for a butcher. Following his marriage to an Irish girl named Mary Bigger, Sloss bought a store in Athens, Alabama. Within a few years, Sloss had become a wealthy businessman and plantation owner. In the 1850s, he became president of the Tennessee and Alabama Central Railroad, which connected Decatur with the Alabama-Tennessee border. In 1871, Sloss merged it with the much larger Louisville and Nashville Railroad. By combining a number of short railroad lines to form a leg of the Louisville and Nashville Railroad, he made it possible to mine and transport the mineral deposits of Jones Valley. Sloss also contributed to the development of the iron industry through his involvement in the purchase of the Red Mountain Coal and Iron Company.

In June 1881, ground was broken for Sloss's new factory on land donated by the Elyton Land Company. He hired a European engineer named Harry Hargreaves. He was a protégé of Thomas Whitwell, who had invented the hot blast stoves being used in factories in Britain. Sloss's domed Whitwell stoves were sixty feet high and eighteen feet in diameter. The principal contractor, J. P. Witherow and Company of New Castle, Pennsylvania, was one of the foremost builders of blast furnaces in the nation. The Linn Ironworks in Birmingham made the blast furnaces that forced air through the furnace at 10,000 cubic feet per minute. The blowing engines with their eighty-four-inch cylinders weighed eighty-five tons. Hargreaves also designed a sixty-foot-tall furnace stack that had a capacity of 80 tons of pig iron per day. Sloss's state-of-the-art furnace differed from the conventional furnaces that had been built near the side of a hill because it was freestanding. The weight of the molten iron and slag was so immense that two separate concrete foundations were built. The first furnace went into blast on April 1, 1882. By the end of the year, it had sold 24,000 tons of iron. Ground was broken for the second furnace on May 1, 1882; construction was completed the next year. The new coal crusher housed in the 500-foot-long stock house was fed coal in a chain of buckets. The crushed coal was then transported to the furnace in five-ton buggies. Coke was used in the making of pig iron because most of Birmingham's trees had been cut down in the early 1870s. The quality of the Sloss Furnaces iron was so high that the Louisville Exposition awarded the company a bronze medal. Most of the pig iron was shipped to Louisville, Cincinnati, Cleveland, and Chicago.

Birmingham was ideally suited for the iron industry because of the thousands of men looking for work. Blacks comprised 65 percent of the Birmingham iron and steel workforce in 1900. The percentage rose to 75 percent in 1910. Cheap labor was so readily available that the owners saw no need to install safety equipment until the 1920s, when thousands of African-Americans were leaving the Deep South in search of better jobs up North. Segregation was as prevalent inside Sloss Furnaces as it was in society at large. Blacks had separate bathhouses, timeclocks, and company picnics. Most of the supervisors and skilled workers were white.

In 1886, John W. Johnston and Forney Johnson purchased Sloss Furnaces from James Withers Sloss. In 1899, the business was reorganized as Sloss-Sheffield Steel and Iron. The company expanded through the acquisition of foundries and coal- and iron-producing lands in northern Alabama. In 1909, James Pickering Dovel improved the design of the furnaces and invented gas cleaning equipment. Between 1927 and 1931, the furnaces were completely refurbished with new equipment. Over the next two decades, the company became one of the largest producers of pig iron in the world. The U.S. Pipe and Foundry Company purchased it in 1952. It changed hands again in 1969 when it was sold to the Jim Walter Corporation. As a result of the Clean Air Act, many of the old smelting works were closed. The Jim Walter Corporation shuttered Sloss Furnaces in 1971 and donated the property to the Alabama State Fair Company for use as an industrial museum. When the authority decided to raze the old iron mill instead, the Sloss Furnace Association was formed to lobby for its preservation. In 1977, a bond issue to maintain the site was passed. Today, Sloss Furnaces is one of Birmingham's most popular attractions, drawing people from all over the South for its concerts, barbecue cook-off, metal-arts classes, Muse of Fire shows, annual ghost tour, and "haunted house," "Sloss Fright Furnace."

The ghost stories of Sloss Furnaces memorialize the workmen who were maimed or killed during its history. Workers' safety was secondary to profits throughout most of the company's operation. Accidents were fairly commonplace, and all but a few of the sixty-seven fatalities have been forgotten. In November 1882, two black workmen—Aleck King and Bob Mayfield—were lowered down on a scaffold into the No. 1 Furnace to chip away at "clinkers" (deposits of ore and coke) that had formed on the inner walls. As they were working away with their pickaxes, one big chunk of ore fell into the furnace, enveloping the two men in clouds of noxious gases. Gasping for breath, the men fell into the furnace. That same week, a despondent employee named Samuel Cunningham climbed to the top of Alice No. 1 and plunged into the flames.

The *New York Times* reported two tragic accidents at the iron mill. The first article recounted the horrible fate that befell a work crew of eight men at Sloss Furnaces. On February 4, 1892, the men were standing on a scaffold while erecting a new hot blast stove. Suddenly, the scaffold collapsed, and all of the men fell eighty-five feet to the bottom. John Staton and John Richie were killed instantly; P. J. Trammell, Job Wade, Will Harvey, Henry Cutts, and Frank Wilcox, and Jerry More were seriously injured. More suffered minor injuries. Another *New York Times* story related the discovery of a young man named Joseph F. Webb in an open water tank on August 4, 1897. He was working as a painter in the local Southern Railway shops at the time. The writer described Webb's injuries in graphic detail: "The body was cooked, and the flesh fell off in chunks as it was drawn from the vat." The cause of the young man's death was never officially determined, although murder was considered a possibility.

Not all of the stories of incidents in the twentieth century can be verified. In the early 1900s, two brothers, Julian and Walker Woods, died in the same week. Julian was suffocated by poison gas, and Walker drowned. Historian and Sloss tour guide Dr. Richard Neely tells the story of a man who was killed in the Blowing Engine No. 1 near one of the sixty-foot-tall steam engines. He used to lean against a particular post each day to eat his lunch. He liked the draft from the nearby flywheel, but when the wheel was operating, it was not safe to stand this close. One day, the wheel snagged and crushed him. "It happened before anybody could blink an eye, and it took them ten minutes to shut the machine down," Neely said. "His body became so mangled as to be unrecognizable." In 1921, Brant Hainsworth was crushed to death by gears in the diesel shed. Around the same time, Noah Tyson was burned to death when molten iron was accidentally poured on him. Dr. Neely suggested that Sloss Furnaces was not overconcerned with the welfare of the workers because they could be easily replaced. "One of the workers I interviewed loved to tell the story that they told the workers here: 'Don't kill any mules. Mules cost twenty-five dollars, but men? Men we can replace.'"

Another unverified story of a death at Sloss Furnaces is believed to have occurred in the early twentieth century. One day while the workers were pouring iron into the sows, a young woman who had become pregnant out of wedlock walked through the gates. Without being noticed, she climbed up Alice No. 1 and leaped into the furnace. Ron Bates, assistant director of Sloss Furnaces, told me that her unquiet spirit returned in a very unusual form. "One day, city officials and plant managers were having some kind of official ceremony at Sloss Furnaces when all at once, a white deer ran through the crowd and disappeared. Some people believed that it was the reincarnation of the pregnant girl who killed herself in the furnace." Bates went on to say that the deer still appears whenever dignitaries visit the furnaces on special occasions.

According to legend, not all of the "accidents" were accidental. One of the most popular—and probably apocryphal—of the Sloss ghost stories revolves around a sadistic foreman named James "Slag" Wormwood. He was hired in the early 1900s to supervise the "graveyard shift" from 9:00 P.M. until 5:00 A.M. Eager to please his employers, Slag pushed the 150 men under his charge, often beyond their limits. It was said that 47 men lost their lives while working the graveyard shift. An untold number were forced to retire because of their injuries. Slag's reign of terror ended in 1906 when he was walking on top of Big Alice, became lightheaded because of the fumes, and fell inside. He died instantly. Soon, rumors spread that one of the workers Slag had tormented for years pushed him into the furnace. Slag's vengeful spirit gave rise to a number of sightings over the years. In 1926, a night watchman said that he was pushed and told to "get back to work." In 1947, three workers who were found unconscious in a boiler room claimed to have been ordered by a spectral voice to get back to work. Another night watchman swore in 1971 that the fiery figure of a man pushed him down the stairs and pummeled him with his fists.

The legend of Slag, which is the basis of the Sloss Fright Furnace event held at the furnaces every October, seems to derive from a horrific death that occurred in 1887 at the DeBardeleben Coal and

Iron Company's Alice No. 1 furnace, not at the Sloss Furnaces. After the Civil War, Theophilus Calvin Jowers left his father's plantation to seek his fortune in Birmingham's iron industry. He married Sarah Latham in Irondale in 1870 and began learning his craft as an ironworker at McElwain's Little Cahaba Iron Works. Three years later, Jowers was hired as an assistant foundry man at the Eureka Mining and Transportation Company of the Oxmoor Furnace. He became the assistant foundry man at Birmingham's Alice No. 1 furnace in the spring of 1887. He was eager to meet the challenge of continuing to produce 150 pigs of iron a day, a record in the South. On September 10, 1887, the Jowers family's dream of a happy, prosperous life in Birmingham came to a tragic end. The plan was to raise the old bell and lower it into the furnace, where it would be melted down. Jowers was holding the rope that was to hoist the bell when he lost his footing and let go of the rope. The massive bell dropped into the molten iron, and Jowers fell on top of it. In a matter of seconds, his body was engulfed and incinerated by the molten iron. In an effort to retrieve Jowers' remains, the work crew attached a gas pipe to a piece of sheet iron and lowered it into the furnace. The men were able to recover his head, bowels, two hip bones, and a few ashes.

Not long after Jowers' death, his coworkers began to suspect that he was fulfilling his promise to his wife: "As long as there's a furnace standing in this county, I'll be there." Men crossing the bridge at Alice were suddenly overcome by a feeling of intense cold. Some men complained about being watched by an unseen presence. Not long thereafter, Jowers' watchful apparition began appearing at Alice No. 1. Workers tending the furnace saw the spectral figure of a man who acted like a supervisor. After Alice No. 1 was demolished in 1905, Jowers seemed to have moved across the street to Alice No. 2. The next sighting of his ghost took place in 1927. His grown son, John Jowers, took his son, Leonard, for a ride to the viaduct on First Avenue in his new Model T Ford. John stopped the car on the viaduct, and he and Leonard walked over to the railing to get a good view of the furnaces. Suddenly, John saw a male figure walking

*Assistant foundryman Theophilus Calvin Jowers fell into Alice No. 1 at Sloss Furnaces.* (Photo from Wikimedia Commons)

through the flames. He directed his son's attention to the spot, but the apparition was gone. For several nights, John returned to the viaduct and watched his father's spirit doing what he loved the most: making iron.

Not surprisingly, other sightings have taken place at the sites where some of the most horrible accidents have occurred. During a 2008 investigation of Sloss Furnaces by members of the *Ghost Adventures* team, an investigator told team leader Zach Bagans that he was slapped in the face while he was filming inside the old iron mill. The group captured an image of mist between two sets of railings and the sound of someone banging metal against metal. Inside the tunnel, the group recorded a child's voice on the video camera. One of the members, Aaron Goodwin, was struck in the eye. Understandably, he was eager to leave Sloss Furnaces.

In 2010, Jason Hawes and Grant Wilson, founders of The Atlantic Paranormal Society (TAPS), heard something run across the catwalk. During the group's EVP session, they asked, "Did you work here?" On the recording, a male voice said, "Yes." Meanwhile, Adam Berry and Amy Bruni were in the Blowing Engine Room, asking questions about working conditions inside the factory, when they heard the rattling of chains. Investigator Meat Loaf set up a laser grid inside the tunnel. After Dave Tango joined him in the tunnel, the two investigators smelled mothballs for a few seconds. Meat Loaf asked, "Did anyone use mothballs?" Almost immediately, a light on the EMF meter turned on, signifying "yes." Wilson was pushed when he was standing in the tunnel. He also heard a spectral voice say, "Hey, look!" Tango and Meat Loaf were in the Blowing Engine Room when they heard the sound of metal banging against metal.

In the investigation conducted by the Tennessee Wraith Chasers on the television series *Ghost Asylum*, Steven "Doogie" McDougal had some unsettling experiences in the Sloss Furnaces. Not long after the investigation began, he was touched on the arm. A few minutes later, he got sick. The shadowy figure of a man blocked the laser grid. The entity took a few steps toward the investigators before finally backing away. By the end of the investigation, the group had captured a mist on film. Even more compelling was the figure of a full-body apparition on the thermal imagery camera. Chris Smith, founder of TWC, proclaimed Sloss Furnaces to be one of the most active places his group has ever investigated.

Not surprisingly, Sloss Fright Furnace is a very popular attraction. In the nineteenth century, Sloss Furnaces produced iron. Today, it produces thrills and chills—of the entertaining variety.

### The Spear-Barter House
### Mobile

The Spear-Barter House at 163 St. Emanuel Street sits next door to the Fort Conde Inn. Isaac Spear built it in 1857 for a local foundry owner. Its red-brick exterior is highlighted with white stucco trim. The windows are small on the left side of the house, where the stairway and hall are located; they are large on the right side, where they overlook the garden. Local legend has it that in its early years, the house served as a brothel. L. D. Spear purchased the house for his wife, Catherine, in 1866. In 1888, she passed it down to her children. Today, the Spear-Barter House is owned and operated by the Posner-Volper Company, which also runs the Fort Conde Inn in Fort Conde Village. The Spear-Barter House is available for rent as office space; one of the rooms is rented out as a honeymoon suite.

Amanda McBride, a desk clerk at the Fort Conde Inn, said that another employee learned the hard way to be respectful to the house's ghosts. "He had heard that the place was haunted. He was skeptical about the ghosts over there, so he used the voice recorder in his phone to collect EVPs. I guess he wanted to prove that the ghosts didn't exist. He asked several questions. Then after a while, he said, 'Why won't you show me you're here? Are you shy?' When he played the recording back, he heard a voice say, 'I'm not bashful.' After that, he refused to sleep over there ever again."

Amanda also had a startling experience in the Spear-Barter House. "I was in the large bedroom that we use as the honeymoon suite. The door was shut. Suddenly, I heard the doorknob shake really hard. It sounded like someone was trying to come into the room. I opened the door, and no one was there. I thought at first that it was the vibration of a train coming by, but it was pretty obvious that somebody was trying to get in."

## Tallassee Community Library
### Tallassee

In 1921, an agent for Mount Vernon-Woodbury Mills, Inc., named J. Ed Harris began developing plans for a public library. It opened in the sunroom of the Scout Club House. Rev. W. E. Bryant, of the East Tallassee Methodist Church, served as librarian. At the time, the library had fewer than two thousand books. The first full-time librarian, Mary Lou Martin, held that position from 1922 until

1948. Ruby Lanier served until 1985, then W. C. Bryant until 1999, when he was succeeded by the current librarian, Sharon Kilpatrick.

The library did not become a bona-fide public library until March 1978, when Tallassee Mills donated it to the city. Just before the transfer, a new wing was added. It housed a museum a while, W. G. Eubanks as director. Thanks to a grant by the Mildred Weedon Blount Educational and Charitable Foundation, Inc., the wing was converted into the Blount Reading and Reference Room in 1989. The library's overall appearance has not changed since it was remodeled in the late 1960s.

Sharon suspected that the Tallassee Community Library was haunted not long after she took the job in 1999. "I'd come in early, around 7:00 A.M. or 7:30 A.M., and I'd notice children's laughter and talking as soon as I walked in the door," she told me in an e-mail. "I'd hear kids running around, a little bit of music. It sounded like a party in there. It didn't bother me, really. A man who used to work here and was normally always here first said he'd heard it too, but he never said anything until I mentioned it to one of the board members while he was listening." Sharon did not really become concerned until a year or so later when she began hearing someone walking around the Children's Room. "One time when I was standing at the front desk—you can see the Children's Room from the front desk—I saw a young man about seventeen or eighteen years old holding the hand of a little five-year-old girl, and they were walking across the room. It's not a small room. They walked into the stacks, and they just disappeared."

A small room within the Children's Room where toys are kept turned out to be haunted as well. On one occasion, Sharon noticed that the rocking horses were rocking by themselves, just as if small children were sitting on them. She distinctly remembered a little boy around two or three years old who stopped on the steps leading to the small room and told his mother, "I don't want to go in there because I don't know those two boys in there." He pointed to the back of the room, but when his mother looked, no one was there.

Sharon said that a male ghost they call the "harmless ham" sits in a rear corner of the main library. The apparition appears to be between twenty and twenty-five years old and is usually dressed in early 1900s clothing. Librarians hear the turning of pages at a table where no one is sitting. They also hear footsteps in the stacks, leading the staff to believe that the ghost is searching for a book. "We've had patrons who've been standing in the aisles looking for books, and they hear somebody come up behind them," Sharon said. One patron felt somebody breathing on her neck. She quickly turned around, but she was alone. Sometimes, the "harmless ham" tries to draw attention to himself in the Children's Room, which was the stage area of the Scout Club House, by stomping his foot, throwing something heavy on the floor, or singing in a soft vice. He has not made many appearances since a few changes were made in the library. "He's noisy, but he has never done anything to make us afraid of him," Sharon said. "I hope he hasn't left. He's our favorite [ghost]."

Another spirit that feels a strong attachment to the library is the ghost of the first full-time librarian, Mary Lou Martin, who worked at the library for twenty-six years. Apparently, she had a reputation of being a "cold" person when she was alive, and she still is after death. "Several of our patrons have experienced cold chills and fear so strong that their hearts feel like they are coming out of their chests while in the room with her portrait," Sharon said. "I admit to having a sudden desire to get out of the room as fast as I can. Sometimes when I open up each morning and walk in, I have hesitated to walk further into the building because of a 'feeling.'" Mary Lou Martin's ghost seems to have moved to the main area of the library. "When no one but the staff is here, we will hear what we think is several bookcases crashing over, making so much noise it's frightening." When the librarians race into the other room, they are surprised to find that everything is in order.

The only full-body apparition that has been sighted in the library is the ghost of a Confederate soldier. Sharon even has a photograph of the spirit. "His shoulders and head are above the bookcase, and you can see him very clearly, and I've got that picture." During an

EVP session held at the library, the soldier gave his name as "Sergeant Fuller." His first name was unintelligible in the recording. "Some people say it's Anthony; some people say it's Augustus," Sharon stated. Other EVPs recorded in the library include "Who's that?" "Where are they going?" and "Help me!"

One of the most active places in the library is downstairs in the Book Sale Room. Sharon said that sometimes, when she opened the door at the top of the stairs, she could hear conversations. "It sounds like everyday people. They're not trying to be quiet. It's mostly male voices that we hear. By the time you get to the bottom of the steps, it's gone. You turn on the light, and there's nobody there."

The location of the Tallassee Community Library could account for some of the haunted activity. "Back in 1832, a house stood here," Sharon said. "Tallassee was just starting to come alive again. The first white man married a Creek woman. They built their house here. When he died, she gave it to the city, and it became a hospital. It was torn down, and this building was built in 1919 on the same land and the same basic area as the house. I think the Civil War soldier might be the ghost of someone who was in the hospital. Some of the apparitions are from the land, not the building. I think the children are from the building because it used to be a community center before it was a library."

## Chapter 4

# Haunted Locations

### Bayview Bridge
### Mulga

The Mulga Bayview Community was the last of several model villages built by the Tennessee Coal and Iron Company in the early 1900s. The houses had between two and five rooms, and they were rented to the workers for two dollars per room per month. In the early years, the community consisted of a doctor's office, schools, churches, parks, and a community center/library. A manmade lake was created when TCI dammed Village Creek. The Bayview Dam is 500 feet high and 90 feet wide and covers over 500 acres. It diverted water to the Ensley Steel Mill four miles away. At the time, the Bayview Dam was considered an engineering marvel. These days, Bayview Bridge, off County Road 269, is known as a good place to find ghosts.

The Bayview Bridge is said to be haunted by the ghost of a lady in white. The residents of Mulga have generated a number of legends to explain her occasional appearance there. In one version, a young woman walked across the bridge late one evening in the 1940s to pick up a wedding dress from the seamstress. On her return trip, she was attacked and killed by a pack of wild dogs or was pushed off the bridge. In another version of the same tale, the woman was a runaway bride. She was driving over the bridge on the night of her wedding when her car suddenly crashed through the railing. Some say that a woman was driving with her young son when she ran off the bridge. She survived, but the little boy died. Her ghost still walks across the bridge, looking for her child. In a variant dating back to the early 1970s, a woman and her baby were drowned when she drove her car off the bridge.

According to witnesses, the Lady in White manifests herself in a number of different ways. Many claim to have seen a transparent woman standing on the bridge, looking down at the water below for her little boy or her bridegroom. Some say that a wet spot in the backseat of their car is evidence that the Lady in White hitched a ride as they were driving across the bridge. Others claim that if you turn off your engine at midnight, the ghost lady will climb into the car and sit next to you on the front seat. Another woman said that her great-grandfather picked up a woman and her baby on the bridge. When he glanced back in the rearview mirror a few minutes later, they were gone. Students from Ensley and Shades Valley High School claim that the ghost ate cookies off the trunks of their cars when they parked on the bridge. Handprints on the rear windows of their cars are proof that she made an appearance.

A concrete bridge replaced the old iron one in 1977. Most of the traffic on the bridge today is made up of curiosity seekers and paranormal investigators. Not surprisingly, some young people have found humor in the tragic story of the Lady in White. For many years, boys have terrified their dates by turning off their cars or trucks on the bridge and waiting for the arrival of the ghost. One young woman put on a long white gown and walked across the bridge to frighten her friends who had driven there to party. Ghosts, it seems, can be funny as well as scary.

## The Boyington Oak
## Mobile

The tragic tale of Charles Boyington is one of Mobile's signature legends. He arrived by ship in Mobile in 1833, on the day the "stars fell on Alabama." Many Alabamians interpreted the meteor shower as a bad sign. For Charles, though, the omen was good—at least, for a while. Not long after disembarking from the ship, he was hired by the printing firm of Pollard and Dale. He also found a room in a boardinghouse owned by Mrs. William George. One of the other boarders, a sickly young man Nathaniel Frost, soon became close friends with Charles. The two often took long walks in Church Street Graveyard, where they sat in the shade of the trees and read the epitaphs on the tombstones. After a couple of months, Charles met a lovely young girl named Rose de Fleur, whose father was Baron de Fleur. Charles was smitten by Rose, and he spent every free moment basking in her beauty, even though her father disapproved of him. As the year reached its end, the couple's love deepened.

In the spring of 1834, Charles' fortunes changed for the worse. First of all, he lost his job at the printing company. Charles feared that the loss of his income would make marriage to Rose impossible. Nathaniel did his best to console his friend, but to no avail. One day, Charles asked Nathaniel, who spent of much his time whittling, to carve a wooden heart for Rose. Nathaniel picked up his knife and a block of walnut, and the two young men set out on one of their weekly walks. At midafternoon, Charles returned to the boardinghouse alone. He gave Mrs. George a package containing the wooden heart and asked her to send it to Rose. Then he boarded the steamship *James Monroe* that evening. The next morning, the body of Nathaniel Frost was discovered in Church Street Graveyard. He had died of several knife wounds to the heart.

Charles was taken into custody aboard the *James Monroe;* he was returned to Mobile on May 16, 1834. Despite his protestations of innocence, a grand jury indicted him for the murder of Nathaniel. His trial was set for November. Even though the evidence against Charles was circumstantial, he was found guilty. The date of his execution was set for February 20, 1835. Charles appealed to the governor for clemency, but he refused to get involved in the case. On the day he was to die, Charles walked behind the cart bearing his coffin. The procession stopped at the gallows on Washington Square, and he mounted its steps. While the Presbyterian minister, William T. Hamilton, spoke words of comfort to Charles, Sheriff

*People in Mobile say that this massive oak tree grew from the grave of convicted murderer Charles Boyington as proof of his innocence.* (Photo from Wikimedia Commons)

Toumlin walked over to a friend of his who was sitting on a log. Suddenly, the sheriff, the sheriff's friend, and the sheriff's horse fell into a dead faint, but they recovered.

As the minister walked slowly down the steps, Charles began to read from a prepared statement. Realizing that Charles was trying to postpone the inevitable, the sheriff ripped the paper from his hand. Undeterred, Charles proclaimed to the crowd that a massive oak tree would grow from his grave as proof of his innocence. His hanging did not go well. The hangman was inexperienced; as a result, Charles struggled at the end of the rope for several agonizing minutes before finally dying.

Charles' body hung from the gallows for thirty minutes before being cut down and placed in the coffin. He was buried in the northwest corner of the Church Street Graveyard, in the potter's field section. For several weeks, people passing by kept a close watch on Charles' grave to see if his prediction had come true. When a tiny oak seedling poked its head out of the ground, hundreds of people made their way to the potter's field to see the fruition of Charles' prophecy. Today, the huge tree that bears Charles' name still stands near the wall on Bayou Street. The potter's field is now a parking lot. Unlike the other poor souls who are buried here, Charles Boyington will always be remembered for the living monument standing over his grave.

### Crybaby Hollow
### Hartselle

Haunted-bridge stories are common throughout the South. Alabama has several of its own, such as the "Bridge at Boyd" in Sumter County, and the Bayview Bridge in Mulga. The most famous of the state's "crybaby bridge" stories involves Crybaby Hollow, located off Highway 31 between Hartselle and Decatur. Kayo Road leading to the bridge is barely wide enough to accommodate two medium-sized vehicles. The one-lane bridge is made of slabs of concrete with no rails. It is approximately twelve feet long. Crossing the bridge at night would be scary enough even without the ghost stories people still tell about Crybaby Hollow.

Several legends have grown up around Hartselle explaining the source of the crying sound people have been hearing for years. The most commonly told tale, which can be found at many other bridge sites as well, concerns an unwed young woman who regrets her socially condemned moment of passion with her boyfriend and tosses the "fruit of her sin" off the bridge in the 1950s. In her book *Haunted North Alabama,* Jessica Penot tells the story of a homicidal maniac who killed a woman and her baby boy and threw their bodies into the creek in the 1940s. Penot traces the beginning of the tale back to the Indians living in the area hundreds of years ago. A woman was combing the hollow for nuts and berries with her baby in tow when they were caught in a thunderstorm. Before she could climb the ravine, a raging flood swept them down the hollow. The woman survived, but her infant was never found. The early Scotch-Irish settlers created their own version of the story. A pioneer family was riding down the road when one of their wagon wheels struck a rock, causing a baby sleeping inside to slide unnoticed off the back end. By the time the child's parents realized she was missing, it was too late. Her wails have echoed through Crybaby Hollow ever since.

Stories of Crybaby Hollow brought this writer to Hartselle in July of 2016. While I was dining at the Freight House Restaurant, a waitress named Karen told me how teenagers in Hartselle summon the ghost baby at the bridge. "You put a candy bar on the back bumper of the car. You walk to the front, and when you come back [to the bumper], there will be teeth marks on it." Karen then told a story about a prank she played on one of her kids at Crybaby Hollow. "I did something bad to one of my kids. Last year, she wanted to go to Crybaby Hollow. She had heard different stories, and she wanted to see if they were true. So we drove out there, and the whole time she was driving to the bridge, I was downloading a ringtone of a crying baby. We were sitting there on the bridge with the windows rolled down. It was just half-dark, and I hit 'play.' Her reaction was really funny." Karen's daughter, who also works as a waitress at the restaurant, recalled another humorous incident at Crybaby Hollow. "My best friend's mom and her boyfriend wanted to go to Crybaby Hollow at night. Three other kids at school and I got in a car with another girl and drove out there first. The adults got out of the car and started walking toward the bridge when they heard voices under the bridge. We were hiding there. We hit the bottom of the bridge, and he ran and ran and ran. It was pretty funny."

### Cuba Railroad Tracks
### Cuba

An aura of mystery surrounds people whose final resting places have never been found. The lives of Alexander the Great, Genghis Khan, and King Arthur have become even more intriguing because their burial sites are unknown, prompting archaeologists and historians to devote their careers to the discovery of their tombs. The unknown burials of people at the fringes of society are even more tragic. For many people, a tombstone is the only remaining record of their having been born. Lacking that final testament to their existence is unimaginable. One lonesome burial site hearkens back to a largely forgotten train wreck in the 1930s.

Cuba artist Linda Munoz learned of this tragic incident when an elderly man named Mitch Cooper walked into the Coleman Center. He approached her and asked if she was Charlie Munoz's wife. When she said that she was, he responded, "Well, I'd like to tell you about something that happened to me back in the Great Depression when I was a little boy." Linda told Mitch that she would like for him and his wife to come to her house so that she could interview him. She said she would also bake a pie for them. A few days later, the Coopers showed up on Linda's doorstep. Charlie and Linda sat in the front parlor with their guests, and Mitch told his story.

"He talked about being a little boy and visiting his grandparents, who lived on the other side of the tracks," Linda said. "He told me that he used to run out to the front porch every time a train rolled by.

On this particular day, he heard the train coming down the tracks. Suddenly, there was this horrible noise. The train jumped the track, and there was this huge explosion. He said that everybody in the area ran down the tracks to see what they could do. They trampled over all of Dr. Beavers' strawberries and green beans." According to an article in the *Meridian Star,* an unknown number of hobos were riding on the train. Many of the men were dead. Some of them were horribly burned; others had lost limbs. One man whose legs had been amputated was brought to Mitch's grandparents' porch, where he bled to death. The writer of the *Meridian Star* article said that the smoke rising from the wreck could be seen as far away as Meridian, Mississippi, twenty miles away. "There were all these maimed and dying people, but there was no way to find out who their relatives were, so they buried them in a trench not too far from the tracks," Linda said. "Mitch showed us the general area where they were buried." It's on the south side of the railroad tracks.

Nothing marks the trench where the men were buried. However, Linda's dogs may have sensed the presence of human remains. "We took our dog Maggie out there," she said. "She would walk around the pines we had down there and sniff around. One time she jumped up, like she was trying to hold me back. This was the only place where she behaved like that. My other dog, Myra, is scared to death down there. She doesn't like the place at all. This happened before Mitch told us the story of the hobos." The dogs' strange behavior could be explained in two ways. Cadaver dogs have been known to find bones hundreds of years old, so it is possible that the dogs had found the remains of people who died over seventy years before. Parapsychologists, on the other hand, would suggest that the dogs may have tuned in to the unquiet spirits of the unfortunate victims of the train derailment.

## East Lake Park
## Birmingham

One of Birmingham's most sensational crimes took place at one of the most tranquil parts of the city: East Lake Park. On December 4, 1888, two men fishing from a boat discovered the body of seven-year-old May Hawes in the water. The subsequent autopsy revealed that little May had been murdered. The prime suspect in the case was her father, Richard, an engineer for the Georgia-Pacific Railroad. The police department's suspicions were aroused when they learned of a newspaper announcement of Hawes' impending marriage to a woman in Mississippi, despite the fact that he was still married to May's mother, a hard-drinking, twenty-eight-year-old woman named Emma. To make matters worse, Emma and May's six-year-old sister, Irene, were missing. When Hawes returned by train to Birmingham with his new wife, he was promptly arrested. Upon learning that her husband was married and had children, Hawes' bride broke down in tears at the train station. A few days later, the bodies of Emma and Irene were found in Lakeview Park waterway. They had been killed with an axe, and their corpses were weighted down with railroad irons. The discovery of a bloodstained axe handle, clothes, and oat sack in the Hawes family home convinced the police that they had arrested the right man. The night after Emma was buried in Oak Hill Cemetery, a lynch mob of 2,000 people converged on the jail, demanding that Hawes be turned over to them. The guards, under orders from Sheriff Joseph S. Smith, opened fire, killing ten citizens, including a young boy. After calm was restored in Birmingham and the trial was able to proceed, Hawes and two accomplices were convicted of murder. Richard Hawes was hanged on February 28, 1890. At the time, this was the most heinous crime ever committed in Alabama. One of the local newspapers called it "The Hawes Horror." Another newspaper gave Birmingham the nickname of "The Murder Capital of the Country."

The ghost of May Hawes still haunts the site of her murder. Her apparition has been seen walking around the perimeter of the lake. Some witnesses have heard the high, trembling voice of a child calling for her mother and sister. The specter of May Hawes is also said to hover over the surface of the lake. Sometimes, the little girl's ghost seems to be partially submerged. A few people claim to have seen the ghostly figure of a girl petting the geese that frequent the park. On Halloween, locals commemorate the spirit of "The East Lake Mermaid" by setting jack-o-lanterns along the shore and casting carnations, May's favorite flowers, into the water.

## The *Eliza Battle*
## Pennington

In the nineteenth century, rivers provided early settlers with a vital link to other states and foreign countries, especially in Alabama. In the 1850s, back when the river channel of the Tombigbee was still deep enough for cotton and pleasure boats to travel most of the year, steamboats were a common sight, carrying passengers and cotton to various landings and cities. One of the finest steamboats from this era was the *Eliza Battle*, whose tragic history invites comparisons with the most infamous luxury boat of the twentieth century, the *Titanic*. Both ships reigned as queens of the water, luxurious transports for the rich and famous, until one dark, cold night, they fell victim to a cruel twist of fate.

The story of the *Eliza Battle* strips away the romantic veneer that has clung to the history of steam boating in America. In the nineteenth century, accidents were as much a part of river life as paddlewheels and smokestacks. High water caused tree-bearing banks to cave in, creating new obstructions. During low water in summer, sandbars became major obstacles. Most steamboat men, however, were not very concerned about sideswiping other ships, because most of these accidents resulted in only minor damage. Submerged logs were responsible for more sunken ships than any other source of danger, although most boats sent to the bottom in this manner were raised or the machinery was transferred to a new hull. But crewmembers and passengers were rarely injured in these mishaps. As a rule, fires cause the most property damage of all the accidents on the river. When one considers that steamboats burned wood or coal to produce steam, and that they hauled highly flammable cargo such as cotton, cottonseed, and cottonseed oil, it is little wonder that fires were fairly common on American rivers. Boiler explosions usually took more lives than fires but were not as common.

Alabama's river history is also marked by tragedy. Steamers often collided with each other on dark, foggy nights or struck snags and sank. Some of these calamities have become memorialized in history books and Alabama river lore. Both of the steamboats named after Alabama's legendary fighter Sam Dale burned in Mobile—*Sam Dale I* in 1852 and *Sam Dale II* in 1856—along with the rifle he used in the famous Canoe Fight. The steamer *St. Nicholas* snagged a sandbar, now known as the "St. Nicholas Bar," near Sunflower, Alabama, in February of 1859 and was lost. On the night of January 9, 1913, the boiler of the *James T. Staples* exploded at Powes Landing near Bladon Springs, killing twenty-six people and injuring twenty-one. *The City of Mobile*, which made weekly trips up the river from Mobile to Selma and was one of the few steamboats built in Mobile, was destroyed by a hurricane, which blew the boat up on the docks in 1916.

Working or riding on the steamboats was also fraught with hazards. Before the Civil War, Irishmen were employed to help slaves with the dangerous work of loading and unloading cotton bales from steamboats because, according to Mell A. Frazer, author of *Early History of Steamboats in Alabama,* it was cheaper for the captain to lose an Irish deckhand than a slave that he owned or had been hired out by his master. Around 1885, a cabin boy aboard the steamboat *Mary* was pushed off the side by 300 cotton bales, which slid overboard. Apparently, it was not much safer to ride on a steamboat. In 1843, Spartan Morrissette, the daughter of a wealthy planter and lawyer, fell off the deck of the *New World* while sleepwalking and drowned. Then around the turn of the twentieth century, a woman and her baby fell off the steamboat *Nettie Quill* and were drowned in the dark waters of the Alabama River, in spite of the efforts of Capt. John Quill to save them.

The *Eliza Battle* was a "regular weekly packet" between Mobile and Warsaw, carrying freight and passengers upriver from Mobile and cotton and passengers downriver from Aberdeen and Columbus, Mississippi. For most of her time on the Tombigbee, the *Eliza Battle* held to the following itinerary, which was published in the January 4, 1853, edition of the *Sumter County Whig.*

*Trip Up-River:*
Leave Mobile every Tuesday evening at 5 o'clock P.M. Tuscahoma Wednesday 9 o'clock A.M., Thompkins' Bluff, James' Bluff, Kemp's Landing & Moscow during the day. Demopolis at 5 o'clock P.M. Bluff Port and Jones' Bluff, Wednesday night. Gainesville Thursday morning. Arrive Warsaw 8 o'clock, same day.

*Return Trip:*
Leave Warsaw 10 o'clock A.M. Thursday. Gainesville, 3 o'clock P.M. Jones' Bluff and Bluff Port early part of that night. Demopolis 12 noon Friday. Moscow and Beckley's Landing, during the day. Kemp's Landing, James' Bluff, Thompkins' Bluff in early part of the night. Tuscahoma at 6 o'clock A.M. On Saturday, Jackson at 3 o'clock P.M. Arrive Mobile Saturday night.

Planters and their families living up and down the Tombigbee often combined business with pleasure as they accompanied their loads of cotton to market in Mobile on the *Eliza Battle.*

The last voyage of the *Eliza Battle,* in late February 1858, was promoted in handbills and newspaper ads as a gala affair for the wealthy and socially prominent. This particular trip was made even more appealing by the inclusion of brightly colored flags and bunting, glowing lanterns, and two bands. The passengers dressed in the style befitting their station in life. Most of the ladies wore full skirts and little hats and carried parasols as protection against the sun's reflection off the water. Newly engaged and married couples anticipated a romantic ride down the moonlit river. The high price that cotton was fetching on the market that year made the atmosphere on the steamboat even more festive, despite the chilly temperatures outside.

After the last bale of cotton had been loaded, one of the bands struck up a dance tune, and the *Eliza Battle* pulled off from the wharf. The band, fortified with spirits against the bracingly cold weather, continued to play all evening, including the Stephen Foster song, "Old Folks at Home." The advertising campaign was so successful that dancing was extremely difficult in the crowded conditions, and meals had to be served on small tables. Nevertheless, as darkness crept upon the river, the *Eliza Battle* stopped at several plantation landings and picked up even more people. After the last couples had boarded at Pickensville, the passenger list swelled to over two hundred people.

Nightfall was accompanied by sleet mixed with snow. The elderly pilot of the *Eliza Battle,* Daniel Epps, was deeply concerned. The extra weight on board the boat had made it sluggish and difficult to steer. Occasionally, the *Eliza Battle* veered off from the main current and piled into the boughs of submerged trees, sweeping cotton bales from the decks. The gloom that had crept inside the pilothouse was lessened somewhat by the sounds of a calliope from another steamer, the *Warrior*, up from Mobile. The *Eliza Battle*'s calliope answered, and for a while the air was filled with the lilting refrain of "Anna Laurie."

Suddenly, above the jubilant sounds of music and laughter and cheering came the cries of "Fire! Fire!" from the stern of the *Eliza Battle*. While crewmembers frantically tried to put out the blaze, Epps called for Capt. S. Graham Stone. After surveying the extent of the damage, Stone entered the ballroom and announced, "Ladies and gentlemen, the boat is on fire." He raised his hand to calm the passengers but to no avail. Women began screaming, and people rushed around looking for the lifeboat, which was inaccessible. Even before most people reached the deck, flames spread from the cotton bales and began engulfing the engine room, cabins, and gangways. As the fire forced the passengers into the bow, some of them contrived makeshift rafts out of bits of lumber and shoved them into the dark water. Others threw cotton bales into the river and tried to climb on top of them. The more daring passengers dived into the water.

In an effort to stay afloat, many grabbed onto the sides of the boat or the limbs of submerged trees, while others ended up drowning. The plummeting winter temperatures made their plight even more desperate.

While bedlam raged on deck and in the water, Captain Stone ordered the pilot to drive the *Eliza Battle* into the riverbank. Epps turned the wheel and discovered to his horror that the tiller rope had been burned completely through. Consequently, the crew could do nothing but stand by helplessly while the steamboat veered toward the trees along the bank and then drifted crazily back toward the current.

After the blazing hull of the *Eliza Battle* drifted downstream, darkness shrouded the scene. Only the screams and prayers of people floundering in the water or holding on to the branches of trees served as a reminder that something terrible had occurred. Fortunately, the glare of the burning boat and the cries of the survivors alerted the citizens of Naheola, and they rushed to the site of the disaster to offer assistance. By dawn, a crowd of local planters were on the bank with their slaves, building rafts that could be guided through the trees with push poles.

Like many tragedies, the burning of the *Eliza Battle* produced several notable heroes. Frank Stone, the boat's eighteen-year-old second clerk, plunged into the icy river and swam ashore holding Mr. and Mrs. Bat Cromwell's young son. He then dived back into the water, placed a Miss Turned on a bale of cotton, and guided it to shore. Unfortunately, he was unable to save the remainder of the girl's family. Her mother died clinging to a tree, and her sister expired in his arms. Another selfless participant in the tragedy was a resident of Naheola named James Eskridge, who piloted a skiff through the undergrowth along the flooded bank in the darkness and saved as many as 100 persons. Most of the people plucked from the freezing water probably would have perished if Rebecca Coleman Pettigrew had not converted her home and outbuildings into a makeshift hospital. For a week, she kept her servants busy hauling in wood and building fires to heat the huge cauldrons of soup that fed the survivors.

After the weather had cleared, the recovery operation began. Because no exact count was kept of the number of bodies pulled from the river, no one knows for sure how many people died on that ill-fated voyage. According to Kathryn Tucker Windham, "Some say twenty-nine, and some say more than fifty." Elizabeth Garth Vestal puts the number at 120. The March 6, 1858, edition of the *Gainesville Independent* reported that 65 people died in the river that night. The *Independent* also published the names of some of the victims:

Dr. S. W. Clanton—Warsaw, Alabama
Mrs. Nancy Cromwell and child—Gainesville, Alabama
William R. T. Smith—Greene County, Alabama
Phil Kirkland—Greene County, Alabama
John D. Willis—Chickasaw, Mississippi
Lewis W. Martin—Fayette County, Kentucky
Mrs. Henry Turned and child—Choctaw County, Alabama
Reverend Mr. Newman—Pickensville, Alabama
John Powell (Barkeep)—*Eliza Battle*
M. A. Galloway—Gainesville, Alabama
Thomas J. Matthews—Yazoo City, Mississippi
Jackson—Barber—*Eliza Battle*
Dargett—Cook—*Eliza Battle*
Nancy—Chambermaid—*Eliza Battle*
Negro—Belonging to B. L. Turner—Choctaw County, Alabama
Robert—Belonging to Colonel T. Buford
Dick—Belonging to Judge Torrey
Jim—Belonging to John Foster
Sam, Peter & Jack—Deck Hands—Belonging to J. A. Mooring
Bill—Belonging to R. G. McMahon
Allen—Belonging to John Bowen
Thirty White Deck Hands were never seen.
The number of blacks lost is reported to have been 10 or 12.
Most of the people who died had frozen after spending between three and four hours in the water.

To this day, no one can say for certain why the *Eliza Battle* burned.

For many years, it was believed that sparks from the chimneys of the *Eliza Battle* or the steamboat that passed her in the night ignited the cotton bales. The March 6, 1858, edition of the *Gainesville Independent* reported that the fire started among the cotton bales and spread to all parts of the boat because of a strong north wind. An interesting footnote to the *Eliza Battle's* tragic end appeared in the February 27, 1975, edition of the *Choctaw Advocate*. In a written confession made to a priest in New York City around 1912, a dying Irishman stated that he and another crewmember aboard the *Eliza Battle* conspired to rob a rich planter who carried a large handbag full of money. After the planter locked the bag in his stateroom and went downstairs to join the other passengers, the two crewmen waited until the boat stopped at Beckley's Landing. Then they broke into the stateroom, set the mattress afire, and took the money. As the crew prepared to cast off, the two thieves disappeared on the bank. The confession was sent to authorities in Mobile, who confirmed it and forwarded the account to the Alabama Department of Archives and History.

The rotting hulk of the *Eliza Battle* is resting in two halves in

*The ghost of the* Eliza Battle *still makes its annual appearance on the Tombigbee River.* (Photo from Wikimedia Commons)

twenty-eight feet of water. Still, the boat occasionally "resurfaces" in oral narratives. In her book *13 Alabama Ghosts and Jeffrey,* Kathryn Tucker Windham wrote, "When the late winter rains send the Tombigbee River out of its banks at Nanafalia, Tuscahoma, Naheola, and Yellow Bluff, there sometimes rises out of the muddy water a ghost ship, the charred hull of a sidewheel steamer. On those stormy nights, some folks along the river say they hear the gay music of a steam calliope, and others report hearing agonizing cries for help blown on the cold river wind." In 1997, a member of the Coast Guard, which operates the locks in Demopolis, told this writer that every February, their office on the Tombigbee receives at least a dozen telephone calls reporting the sighting of the burning hulk of a steamboat on the river. While it is likely that the imaginations of these eyewitnesses have been bolstered by Ms. Windham's account, the fact remains that the *Eliza Battle*'s sad legacy lives on in the collective memory of Alabamians.

## The Harrison Cemetery
## Kinston

William "Grancer" Harrison was born in 1789 in Edgefield County, South Carolina. In the 1830s, he moved his family and slaves to Coffee County, Alabama, and established a plantation on a high bank overlooking the Pea River, not far from what is now Kinston. Because the flood of 1929 wiped out the courthouse, specifics regarding Harrison's life are unknown. For example, no one knows for sure if he lived in a fine Greek Revival mansion like the ones preferred by most planters at the time or in a one-story log cabin. His farm soon became a highly successful enterprise. His bountiful cotton and corn crops were the envy of all of the other planters in the region. Although Harrison was proud of his agricultural achievements, his real passion was the social activities he hosted. Every Saturday night, he entertained his neighbors with horseraces and barbecues. To cement his home's reputation as the social center of the county, he had his slaves build a large dancehall on his property. He enjoyed buck dancing across the waxed floor in his custom-made shoes and suit.

Grancer, as his grandchildren called him, began thinking more and more about death as he grew older. Shortly before he died, he had his slaves bring back bricks from Milton, Florida, and build him an impressive aboveground tomb. He gave his family explicit instructions to dress his corpse in his dancing clothes and his clogs. He also wanted to be laid out on his featherbed and carried to his tomb. He had his final resting place built close to his dancehall so that he could still feel connected to it. His directions were followed to the letter.

The dances continued for a while after his death. However, the big weekend frolics were not as much fun without Grancer, so people stopped attending them. Not long thereafter, people passing by the

*Passersby have heard the melodious strains of fiddle music coming from Grancer Harrison's tomb.* (Photo from Wikimedia Commons)

Harrison Cemetery claimed to have heard the pounding of dancing feet and energetic renditions of old-time fiddler tunes. Some even heard a booming male voice calling out square dances.

Harrison's tomb has been vandalized and rebuilt several times. It was originally covered by a large, wooden grave shelter, but it has long since rotted away. The last time the tomb was rebuilt was in 2005. Unfortunately, it was vandalized again five years later. Harrison's tomb may have incurred considerable damage over the years, but his legendary love of dancing persists to the present day.

## Huggin' Molly
### Abbeville

The Huggin' Molly tale may have had its roots in two stories that were told in Abbeville in the 1890s. One of them concerned a "woman in black" who, it is said, was the spirit of an unwed mother poisoned, allegedly, by the child's father. The other story centered around the ghost of a man who died in prison. "The man in black," as he was called, roamed the streets of Abbeville in a futile attempt to be reunited with his family.

Huggin' Molly as a character did not appear until the early twentieth century. She was said to be a seven-foot-tall phantom who was "as big around as a bale of cotton." People claimed she stalked her victims and crushed them in her strong embrace. She lived in a dark alley behind the schoolhouse. For generations, children and even teenagers scurried home from school to avoid running into Huggin' Molly. Some variants of the tale seem to be preventative in nature. Many parents and grandparents told children that Huggin' Molly would hug them and scream in their ear if she caught them walking around after curfew. Jimmy Rane, who has lived in Abbeville all his life, said his fear of Huggin' Molly was instilled in him by friends and relatives. "If your mother or dad didn't want you to be out after dark, they'd tell you Huggin' Molly would get you. And you believed it, too." The father of Rane's childhood friend Tommy

Murphy added credibility to the folktale by telling the boys that he had actually been hugged by Huggin' Molly one moonlit night.

Even though the Huggin' Molly stories seem to belong in the category of cautionary folktales, a number of encounters with the creature have been recorded. One of these tales was told by Mack Gregory, who was fifty-nine years old when his interview was recorded in 1960. At the time of his paranormal experience, he was a teenager working at Lawson Gregory Grocery Store. He said that early one Saturday evening, he had just finished delivering groceries and was walking home on East Washington Street. As daylight faded away, he realized that someone was walking behind him, keeping pace with his footsteps. With the stories he had heard all his life about Huggin' Molly echoing in his head, he finally summoned the courage to look behind him. Even in the dim light, he could make out the form of a black-robed figure. Mack quickened his pace when his house came into view. When he was a block away from home, he began running as fast as he could. Mack bounded up the steps, threw open the front door, and dashed inside, panting heavily. He was convinced that he had made the acquaintance of Abbeville's spectral stalker.

Marian Glover Leonard, who was born in Abbeville in 1916, recounted the story of another teenager's terrifying run-in with Huggin' Molly. James Robert Shell, her next-door neighbor, told her that one evening, he was walking back to his house on the corner of Elm and Clendinen streets. All of a sudden, he sensed that someone was walking behind him. He spun around and was shocked to see a huge figure in a black robe following him. When he was approximately one hundred yards away from home, Shell broke into a sprint. His mother was standing on the porch, holding the front door open and yelling, "Run, Robert—run!" Thanks to her, Shell was barely able to escape the clutches of the fiend of Abbeville.

Today, the very identity of this little wiregrass community has been fused with the legend of Huggin' Molly. The sign that welcomes visitors to the town features the silhouettes of large woman wearing a long, billowing skirt chasing a little boy. The town's best-known

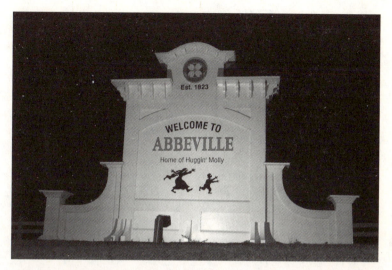

*Generations of children have come home before curfew in Abbeville because of the legend of Huggin' Molly.* (Courtesy Marilyn Brown)

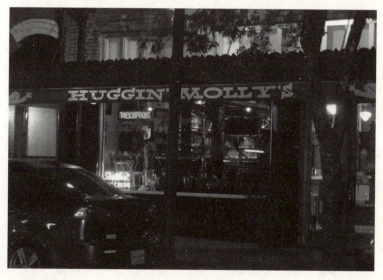

*Huggin' Molly's restaurant takes its name from the Abbeville phantom.* (Courtesy Marilyn Brown)

eatery, Huggin' Molly's, offers diners home-cooked cuisine and a large helping of nightmarish tales about Abbeville's most famous legend.

### Maple Hill Cemetery
### Huntsville

On September 14, 1822, a wealthy planter named LeRoy Pope sold two acres to the city of Huntsville for use as a cemetery. Evidence suggests that settlers had used the plot of land as an unofficial burial ground for years. Most of the grave markers in this section of present-day Maple Hill Cemetery have deteriorated. An exception is the grave of Mary Frances Atwood, who died in infancy on September 17, 1820. Two more acres were added to the cemetery in 1849. During the Civil War, 187 unknown Confederate soldiers were buried in the north side of the graveyard; an undetermined number of Union soldiers were interred throughout. In 1873, Hebrew and Catholic sections were added. Maple Hill Cemetery acquired more land in 1881 and 1903. With funds donated by a wealthy man named Albert Russel Erskine, the stone entrance and the road leading to the Erskine mausoleum were constructed. He also donated twelve acres he purchased from a residential development. The addition of fifty-nine acres tripled the size of the cemetery.

Aside from being the oldest graveyard in Huntsville, Maple Hill Cemetery is one of the most haunted cemeteries in the state. One of the governors buried here is Thomas Bibb. During an 1839 stay in New Orleans, he became ill and died. According to legend, his corpse was placed in a barrel of whiskey to preserve it for the long trip back to Huntsville. The governor's body was originally buried on the family farm at Belle Mina, but for some reason, the family decided to relocate the burial site to Maple Hill. Apparently, the governor's spirit was not pleased with his final resting place, because people have frequently reported seeing a somber black carriage drawn by black horses leaving the cemetery at sunset.

*Gov. Thomas Bibb's ghost is still unhappy about being interred in Maple Hill Cemetery.* (Photo from Wikimedia Commons)

Thomas Bibb's daughter-in-law, Mary Chambers Bibb, is not resting in peace either. In the weeks preceding her wedding day, she bleached her skin by applying a mixture of arsenic and carbolic acid. Just before her wedding, she accidentally ingested carbolic acid and died three months later, on May 26, 1835. Her grief-stricken husband interred her in an elaborate, Greek Revival-style mausoleum. Soon afterward, a housekeeper for the Bibbs spread the rumor that Mary had been buried sitting upright in her favorite rocking chair. Over time, the legend arose that if you walk up to the tomb and knock on its walls, you can hear the creaking sound of Mary's chair as she rocks back and forth.

Another haunted mausoleum in Maple Hill Cemetery is that of the Erskine family, which is not only the largest but has also generated the best-known recent legend about the graveyard. Albert Russel Erskine, former president of Studebaker Motors, was one of the last of the Erskines to be interred here. He shot himself in 1933 after losing all of his money in the stock-market crash of 1929. The story goes that if you drive from the main entrance toward the monument, you can see the image of an angel materialize on the door. However, this ghostly phenomenon can be explained away scientifically. Over the years, the metal of the door has oxidized in a pattern that, when touched by light, produces this effect.

The strangest ghost story associated with Maple Hill Cemetery concerns Maple Hill Park, which is not really part of the graveyard. The most haunted part of the 8.64-acre park is the playground. Locals say that at night, after the park has closed, this secluded place becomes the domain of the ghosts of children. The swings seem to move back and forth by themselves, even on days with no breeze. In her book *Haunted North Alabama*, author Jessica Penot recounted the experience of a group of paranormal investigators in the park. Leilani, a member of the Alabama Paranormal Society, said that she saw the ghost of a woman wearing a Victorian-era dress. Her group concluded that the ghostly children who play in the park after hours are the spirits of children buried in Maple Hill Cemetery. In 2007, a plan to expand the graveyard even further through the acquisition of the adjoining city park, where the playground is located, was eventually shelved because of the public outcry. For the time being, at least, it appears that the little spirits will continue to enjoy their eternal childhood in Maple Hill Park.

## Old Cahawba Archaeological Park
### Orrville

Alabama achieved statehood following the Creek War of 1813-14 and the Treaty of Fort Jackson. Because the rivers were natural highways for the early settlers, the state capital was located at the confluence of the Cahaba and Alabama rivers. After the town was surveyed and the capitol building was constructed, Cahawba became the official state capital in 1820.

However, the frequent floods, abundance of mosquitoes, and regular outbreaks of swamp fever made Cahawba totally unsuitable as the capital. Six years later, Tuscaloosa became the state capital. The residents of Cahawba adapted to the loss of their town's prestige by converting their town into a river port.

Soon, steamboats began picking up bales of cotton at Cahawba. The town's population grew to over three thousand after the arrival of the railroad in 1859, but Cahawba's prosperity proved to be short-lived. By 1863, its business prospects declined as a result of the Union blockade of the coast and the removal of the iron rails from the railroad tracks. Ironically, the Civil War then restored Cahawba's fortunes. In 1863, a cotton warehouse was converted to the Cahawba Military Prison, known locally as Castle Morgan. As many as three thousand Union prisoners lived in cramped conditions and subsisted on meager food rations. Amazingly, Castle Morgan's death rate—2 percent—was one of the lowest in both the Federal and the Confederate prison systems. After the prisoners were released toward the end of the Civil War, over two thousand of them perished when the steamboat they were being transported on exploded on April 27, 1865. Cahawba's fate was sealed a few months later when a devastating flood washed away much of the town. In his book *At Cahaba*, Daniel Meador says that the abandoned houses, stores, and other structures remained standing long after the town's inhabitants left. Eventually, most of the buildings either collapsed or were torn down by their owners. "The structures diminished decade by decade, but one observer reported that in the 1890s, there were still some 150 remaining in various states of dilapidation." Meador surmises that by1910, most of the remnants of Old Cahawba were gone. Over the next few decades, Cahawba's few remaining residents were replaced by birds and other animals. In 1975, the Alabama Historical Commission assumed authority over the site, and in 1989, it was unincorporated, making it a ghost town. Today, the commission runs the Old Cahawba Archaeological Park, which includes collapsed cellars, the Barker Slave Quarters, artesian wells, crumbling foundations, chimney ruins, church, and old cemeteries.

Ghosts are as much a part of the fabric of Old Cahawba as are the nature trail and welcome center. Old Cahawba's oldest ghost story is the tale of Pegues' Ghost. According to Kathryn Tucker Windham, author of *13 Alabama Ghosts and Jeffrey*, in 1862 a young Confederate officer and his girlfriend were walking through the maze of thick cedars standing behind the home of Col. C. C. Pegues, who had been killed in Virginia. Suddenly, a glowing ball of light appeared in front of them. Hovering a few feet off the ground, the light moved from side to side before darting into the shadows. After a few seconds, the light reappeared right beside the couple. As the ball continued zigzagging among the cedars, the soldier decided to attempt to catch it the next time it was close enough. They had walked only a few steps when the illuminated ball appeared right in front of them. The young man made a lunge for the glowing object, but it vanished. Over the next few weeks, several other people who had strolled into the cedars caught sight of the strange ball of light.

The oldest original structure in Old Cahawba—the Fambro/Arthur Home—is said to be haunted by one of the original owners. It was assembled from two older homes by Judge W. W. Fambro. His wife, Elizabeth, was twenty-eight years old when she married the forty-five-year-old judge. The couple had no children, but they opened their house to students and teachers who needed a place to stay. In 2016, a man rushed into the welcome center and said, "I saw it—I saw a lady walking outside of the Fambro House!" When he calmed down, he remarked that she resembled the woman in the photograph on the sign in front of the home. A fence prohibits visitors from accessing the house.

Ghost sightings have also occurred at the New Cemetery. All of the burials date from 1848 to 1900. Many of the people interred here succumbed to yellow fever. The most famous grave in the New Cemetery is that of John A. Bell. On May 23, 1856, John R. Bell and his two sons were engaged in a shootout in the streets of Old Cahawba with Will E. Bird, Thomas Hunter, and Mathew Troy. The Bells were accused of training one of their slaves named Pleas to steal keys and rob houses. John R. and John A. Bell were killed, but none of their assailants was found guilty. The inscription on the grave of John A. Bell suggests that the Bell family disagreed with the verdict: "No murder hath eternal life abiding in him." Some visitors and park employees believe that the violent deaths of citizens and Civil War soldiers buried there have left a psychic imprint on the land. In 2016, a maintenance man claimed to have seen the apparition of a woman in a long, Victorian-era dress walking through the cemetery. His girlfriend recorded the image on her cellphone. Interestingly enough, most of the full-body apparitions appear in the daytime.

Linda Derry, the director of Old Cahawba, had a ghostly encounter in the New Cemetery at the base of the Bell family monument in the late 1990s. She was accompanying a group of investigators from Central Alabama Paranormal Investigations who were spending the night in the park. Derry was walking through the cemetery late that night when the investigators waved her over to the Bell monument. They played back an EVP of a voice that said, "Don key." Don was the maintenance manager of the park. The next morning, he complained to Derry that he could not find his keys anywhere. Later in the day, they were found in the slave cemetery near the grave of the slave who was accused of stealing keys for the Bell family.

One of the buildings that the group investigated that night was the Barker Slave Quarters, built by Stephen Barker in 1860. After the war, the Kirkpatrick family lived on this property. One of the members of the family, Clifton Kirkpatrick Meador, visited his grandparents in Old Cahawba in 1936 when he was five years old. In 1989, he captured his memories of that summer in a poem. Clifton remembered being told several times by a man named Gat, probably an ex-slave, to be careful around the Alabama River because Herbert Kirkpatrick had drowned there in 1879 at age ten. In the poem, Gat gives Clifton some other words of advice. For example, he tells Clifton "Don't never walk across no grave/'cause they reach up and get you." In a note at the end of the poem, Clifton says that Gat had died several years before Clifton was born and that he "falsely believed that Gat still existed." The implication is that Gat was Clifton's protective spirit.

In 2013, the cast of the Syfy television series *Deep South Paranormal* visited Old Cahawba. They conducted the investigation quickly because the river was rising. They broke up into two groups

*The Barker Slave Quarters survived after the Kirkpatrick mansion burned down in 1935.* (Photo from Wikimedia Commons)

in order to cover more ground in a short period of time. Randy Hardy and Hart Fortenbery investigated the cemetery. At the same time that they heard footsteps, Kali Hardy at base camp saw the image of a face in a pool of water. Hart decided that the best way to make contact with the dead was to build a coffin and place Randy inside of it. The next day, Randy climbed inside the newly built coffin. Hart gave him a necklace with a vial of snake venom. He also instructed Randy to place dandelion blossoms over his eyes to help summon the spirits. After the lid was placed on the coffin, Randy recited the following incantation: "Take from these witches' flowers and bring the dead to these living hours." Randy soon complained in his walkie-talkie of having trouble breathing. He said that it felt as if something was sitting on his chest when he repeated the incantation. He also heard something make a noise by his head. After Randy was released, Hart said that he saw a glowing figure standing in the distance behind the coffin.

*While investigating the Barker Slave Quarters, paranormal investigators heard scratching sounds and the rattling of a chain.* (Courtesy Marilyn Brown)

Benny Reed, Keith Ramsey, and Jonathan Hodges investigated the Barker Slave Quarters. At 1:13 A.M., they heard scratching sounds and the rattling of a chain outside the house.

Derry said, "The spirit of the past is not going to hold still." Some would argue that her prediction has come true. In 2016, two ladies who claimed to have psychic abilities returned to the welcome center after their self-guided tour and told the clerk at the desk that Old Cahawba was "full of spirits." The experiences of the *Deep South Paranormal* cast and others would seem to support these statements.

## The Sucarnoochee River
### Livingston

Steve Renfroe is one of Sumter County's most notorious characters. He was a tall, dashing man who was very popular with the ladies. In fact, he was married three times. Reconstruction was well in place when Renfroe arrived from Lowndes County in 1868 after shooting his brother-in-law in a squabble over some chickens the year before. His hatred for carpetbaggers and blacks soon catapulted him into prominence. Through his wife's family connections, he became a member of the Ku Klux Klan. Renfroe and his cronies were instrumental in the persecution of local blacks, the disappearance of a Republican judge, and the murder of the bodyguard of a local magistrate. A jury found Renfroe innocent in the murder of a carpetbagger named Billings in 1874. Four years later, Renfroe was elected sheriff of Sumter County. Children loved him, blacks feared him, and women adored him.

Renfroe proved to be a poor administrator. He was eventually arrested for embezzlement of county funds and thrown into the same jail where he had incarcerated many an offender. That night, though, he managed to set all of the prisoners free. The next day, he burned down the circuit clerk's office, which contained his indictment papers. He still had quite a few loyal friends, and they gave him a large sum of money in the hope that he would start over somewhere else. Instead, Renfroe rode around the town square on his white horse, just as tall and arrogant as ever. He was rearrested and put back in jail. But when the jailer discovered that the bars in Renfroe's window had been nearly cut through with a hacksaw, the prisoner was transferred to a jail in Tuscaloosa that was supposed to be much stronger. It wasn't. Renfroe burned a hole in the eighteen-inch-thick floor and escaped. A few days later, he fled to Slidell, Louisiana, on a stolen mule and saddle. He was captured there and returned to Livingston, where he was sentenced to hard labor in the mines of the Pratt Coal and Iron Company in Birmingham.

In less than sixty days, Renfroe escaped again. The guards tracked him with bloodhounds, but he eluded them by walking backward down a creek. He eventually made his way to the "Flat Woods" between Livingston and the Mississippi border, and this became his headquarters. From there, Renfroe proceeded to rob plantation homes and houses in small towns. Some of the people he robbed were his former friends. He persuaded some of the blacks in the area to cut him a road through the woods to Mississippi so that whenever a posse pursued him, he could run to the state line for safety. So many crimes were credited to him that he kidnapped a reporter for the *Montgomery Advertiser* named Sidney Smith and gave him a special interview in the Flat Woods. Renfroe said, "If I did everything that I am accused of doing, I'd be a very busy fellow. All I have come back for this time is to raise money enough to go to South America and leave this country forever. The only thing I hold against anybody is putting stripes on me and dogs on my tracks." Renfroe never did make it to South America, probably because he could never stay away from Livingston for long. Carl Carmer in his book *Stars Fell on Alabama* speculates that Renfroe loved Livingston because it was the scene of his former triumphs. Inevitably, it was his fondness for Livingston that led to his death.

The events directly preceding and following Renfroe's capture and death are shrouded in mystery, primarily because the people involved wanted their identity to remain a secret. In fact, the only witnesses willing to talk were children at the time, and they were reluctant to say anything until almost half a century later. For example, Ruby Pickens Tartt—who was Alabama's greatest collector of folksongs and folklore in the 1930s—told Carmer in 1934 that Renfroe came to visit her father, William King Pickens, shortly before he was captured. At this time, Miss Ruby was only six years old, and she did not catch everything her parents talked about, but she did remember her father saying to her mother, "It's Steve. He will not hurt me. He's my friend." Ruby's mother gathered that Renfroe was asking her husband what would happen to him if he gave himself up. However, some people in Livingston still believe that Renfroe had threatened to turn the names of local Ku Klux Klan members over to the federal government if Mr. Pickens and his friends did not raise a large sum of money for him. Whatever Mr. Pickens told Renfroe, it must have been pretty discouraging, because that same night a mule belonging to Renfroe's brother-in-law disappeared, along with the silverware belonging to a kindly lady that he had boarded with years before.

A few days later, three Mississippi farmers read in the local newspaper about the theft of the mule and silverware and about the $440 reward on Renfroe's head. They had heard than an unidentified man had been seen stopping at the house of a black man in Enterprise, Mississippi. They went to see the man, and he promised to notify the farmers the next time the stranger came to stay with him. Then on Saturday, July 10, 1886, Renfroe appeared on his doorstep. As soon as he left, the black man told the three farmers, and they took off in pursuit. They caught up with Renfroe on Sunday afternoon at one o'clock. The men moved ahead of Renfroe and lay in wait. Renfroe ambled up on horseback, holding an umbrella. Before he could draw his Navy Six, one of the men fired a load of birdshot into Renfroe's back and side. They accidentally shot the mule too, and he reared up, threw Renfroe to the ground, and ran off. Renfroe was not seriously injured, even though he had sixty pellets in his back, and he was taken sixty miles south to Enterprise. From there, he was moved to the Livingston jail.

At 8:30 P.M. on Tuesday, July 13, a group of men appeared before the jail. They seized the jailer's keys, grabbed Renfroe, and formed a procession that marched through lower Livingston. This must have been a very strange sight because none of the men said a word to each other, and none of the citizens seemed to take notice. They took the road through a cow pasture and halted at the bank of the Sucarnoochee River. Renfroe was then hauled to a large chinaberry tree. When the end of a rope was thrown around an overhanging tree limb, someone asked him if he wanted to pray, and he said, "Boys, you know I ain't never prayed a day in my life." He added, though, that if someone wanted to pray for him, he could. While the members of the lynch mob bowed their heads, the leader said, "God, have mercy on the soul of this miserable man." Renfroe was then pulled clear of the ground, and the rope was tied to a smaller tree. Before leaving, they attached a placard to his back that read, "The fate of a horse thief." Meanwhile, the jailer alerted Sheriff McCormick of the lynching, but by the time they reached the river, it was too late. They cut down his corpse and took it back to town.

The legend of Steve Renfroe's ghost sprang up soon after his body was placed on a cot in the hallway of the Sumter County Courthouse. According to eyewitnesses, a green glow illuminated the rotunda that evening. He was not given a funeral, and there were no mourners. Because Renfroe was an outlaw, he could not be buried in the Livingston Cemetery's hallowed ground, so his corpse was carried to the other side of the fence and buried in a potter's field in an unmarked grave. The story goes that a few years later, this site became the town dump, so one night, his brother-in-law sneaked in, dug up Renfroe's corpse, and took him to Old Side Cemetery near Epes. He buried Renfroe between two of his wives, Mollie and Mary.

Renfroe's legend lives on in the town's ghost lore. In *Stars Fell on Alabama,* Carmer says that every July 13, dark clouds form in the sky over the Sucarnoochee. When the wind begins to howl, Renfroe's ghost, sitting astride his horse, Death, rides out of the clouds.

*The ghost of the outlaw sheriff of Sumter County, Steve Renfroe, reappears over the Sucarnoochee River every July 13, the anniversary of his lynching.* (Photo by Alan Brown)

Renfroe's ghost swoops over the river and flies back into the clouds. The chinaberry tree from which Renfroe was lynched is also said to be haunted. For years, blacks and whites reported that cows would not rest in its shade, and birds would not alight on its branches. The most commonly told story about Renfroe's tree was collected by Ruby Pickens Tartt in an ex-slave narrative by Henry Gary: "People say that if you go up to the tree and say, 'Renfroe, Renfroe. What did you do?' the tree says right back at you, 'Nothing.'"

## USS *Alabama*
## Mobile

The keel of the USS *Alabama* (BB-60), a South Dakota-class battleship, was laid at the Norfolk Navy Yard in Portsmouth, Virginia, on February 1, 1940. Its sponsor was Henrietta McCormick Hill, the wife of J. Lister Hill, the senior senator from Alabama. The battleship was commissioned on August 16, 1942, with Capt. George B. Wilson in command. Its shakedown training began on November 11 in Chesapeake Bay.

Following a ten-day overhaul at Norfolk, the *Alabama* reported for duty with the Third Fleet at Efate, New Hebrides, in September 1943. The ship had its first taste of battle in the Gilbert Islands in November and December. Along with units of Task Force 58, the *Alabama* attacked Truk in the Carolines. The battleship shot down a Japanese Betty on March 29, 1944. On April 21-24, the *Alabama* supported Gen. Douglas MacArthur's troops along the north coast of New Guinea. It bombarded Ponape and Truk on April 29-30. On June 13, the *Alabama* and the rest of the fleet participated in the six-hour pre-invasion bombardment of the western coast of Saipan. As the assault moved ashore two days late, the battleship downed another Japanese plane. After bombarding the Marianas, the *Alabama* sailed on to Guam in July for pre-invasion support. It assisted with the capture of the Southern Carolines in September. The battleship and a number of aircraft carriers destroyed Japanese installations in Formosa, the Philippines, the Pescadores, and the Ryukyu Islands. As part of Adm. William F. Halsey's fleet, the *Alabama* fought in the Battle of Leyte Gulf. It underwent an extensive overhaul in December. After leaving the shipyard, the battleship joined the Third and Fifth fleets in attacking the Japanese home islands on the Okinawa Gunto. On May 4, 1945, the *Alabama* shot down two kamikaze planes. A typhoon inflicted slight damage on the battleship on June 5. On July 17, the *Alabama* bombarded the mills and factories on Honshu Island.

The *Alabama* also did its part to smooth the U.S. Navy's transition to peacetime. On September 20, 1945, the ship departed Japanese waters and would return 3,700 veterans to the U.S. On October 27, the *Alabama* celebrated Navy Day in San Francisco.

The battleship was decommissioned on January 9, 1947, and mothballed in Puget Sound at Bremerton. Plans to scrap the *Alabama* in 1962 sparked a campaign to return the "Mighty A" to Alabama. It began with Alabama schoolchildren raising $100,000 in nickels, dimes, and quarters. Corporate fundraising generated the balance of the $1 million required for the U.S. Navy to donate the ship. The *Alabama* was opened as a museum ship in Mobile Bay on January 9, 1965.

Violent death became part of the old battleship's legacy in 1942 when two men died in the Norfolk shipyard. In its thirty-seven months of service, the *Alabama* suffered no deaths from enemy fire. However, eight sailors died when safety features failed and gun turret #9 fired on gun turret #5. The men were reduced to bits of bone and flesh; all that remained of the gun commander was his boots.

Although most employees of Battleship Memorial Park deny that the *Alabama* is haunted, the testimony of visitors says otherwise. Visitors report seeing the ghostly images of sailors in the officer's quarters and cook's galley. People have heard weird tapping sounds, big-band music, disembodied voices, and phantom footsteps on the ship. Bulkhead doors have been known to open and close by themselves. One of the cub scouts spending the night on the ship saw a barefoot sailor standing by turret #5. Orbs have been captured

*The ghost of a sailor killed by "friendly fire," Matthew Trojan, is said to haunt the sick bay on the USS Alabama. (Photo from Wikimedia Commons)*

in photographs taken aboard the *Alabama,* and balls of light have been seen floating around.

One of the haunted places on the ship is the brig, where a Japanese prisoner committed suicide. The spirits of dead and wounded sailors are said to haunt the wardroom, which served as a triage station during the war. The sick bay may be haunted by the ghost of Matthew Trojan, a victim of the gun turret #5 tragedy. The ghost of a worker killed at the Norfolk shipyard may be making its presence known at the port-side quarterdeck. Unknown spirits also seem to be frequenting the passageways and CPO Lounge.

# Bibliography

## Books

Booth, Donna. *Alabama Cemeteries*. Birmingham: Crane Hill, 1999.

Brown, Alan. *Haunted Birmingham*. Charleston: History Press, 2009.

Carmer, Carl. *Stars Fell on Alabama*. Tuscaloosa: University of Alabama Press, 1989.

Ellison, Rhoda Coleman. *History of Huntingdon College, 1854-1954*. Montgomery: New South Books, 2004.

England, Bob, Jack Friend, Michael Baily, and Blanton Blankenship. *Images of America: Fort Morgan*. Charleston: Arcadia Press, 2000.

Gamble, Robert. *The Alabama Catalog: A Guide to the Early Architecture of the State*. Tuscaloosa: University of Alabama Press, 1986.

Haveman, Chris. *Rivers of Sand: Creek Indian Emigration, Relocation, and Ethnic Cleansing in the American South*. Lincoln: University of Nebraska Press, 2016.

Higdon, David, and Brett Talley. *Haunted Alabama Black Belt*. Charleston: History Press, 2013.

Lewis, W. David. *Sloss Furnaces and the Rise of the Birmingham District*. Tuscaloosa: University of Alabama Press, 1994.

Marengo County Heritage Book Committee, ed. *The Heritage of Marengo County, Alabama*. Clanton, AL: Heritage Publishing Consultants, 2000.

Mead, Robin. *Haunted Hotels*. Nashville: Rutledge Hill Press, 1995.

Meador, Daniel J. *At Cahaba: From Civil War to Great Depression*. Brule, WI: Cable, 2009.

Ossman, Laurie. *Houses of the South*. New York: Rizzoli International, 2010.

Ownes, Harry P. *Steamboats and the Cotton Economy*. Jackson: University Press of Mississippi, 1990.

Painter, Kathy, and Anne Thibodeaux. *Steamboats A-landin'*. Monroeville, AL: Monroe County Heritage Museum, 1992.

Parker, Elizabeth. *Mobile Ghosts: Alabama's Haunted Port City*. Mobile: Apparition, 2001.

Penot, Jessica. *Haunted North Alabama*. Charleston: History Press, 2010.

Roberts, Nancy. *Haunted Houses: Tales from 30 Haunted Homes*. Chester, CT: Globe Pequot Press, 1988.

Serafin, Faith, et al. *Haunted Auburn and Opelika*. Charleston: History Press, 2011.

Severen, Kenneth. *350 Years of Distinctive American Buildings*. New York: E. P. Dutton, 1981.

Shannonhouse, Edna Morrissette. *The Morrissettes of North Carolina and Other States*. Elizabeth City, NC: Rapier and Associates, 1972.

Turnage, Sheila. *Haunted Inns of the Southeast*. Winston-Salem, NC: John F. Blair, Publishers, 2001.

Windham, Kathryn Tucker. *The Ghost in the Sloss Furnaces*. Birmingham: Birmingham Historical Society, 1978.

———.*Jeffrey's Latest 13: More Alabama Ghosts*. Tuscaloosa: University of Alabama Press, 1982.

———.*13 Alabama Ghosts and Jeffrey*. Tuscaloosa: University of Alabama Press, 1969.

## Magazine Articles

McLendon, Nancy Gregory, "Phantoms of the Wiregrass: Tracing the Incarnations of Alabama Folklore." *Alabama Heritage* (Fall 2011).

Vestal, Elizabeth Garth. "Terror on the *Eliza Battle*." *Dixieland/This Week* (October 5, 1969).

## Newspapers

Buckner, Brett. "Oh, to be Yonge again: Some say haunting spirit returns to place of brutal death." *Opelika-Auburn News,* January 23, 2000.

Brown, Jennifer Jacob. "Haunted Places: Livingston's Lakewood House." *Meridian Star,* October 31, 2009.

————. "Haunted Places of East Mississippi and West Alabama: The House on Baldwin Hill." *Meridian Star,* October 31, 2008.

*Choctaw Advocate,* February 27, 1975.

Cobb, Mark Hughes. "Digging up the through about the Jemison house." *Tuscaloosa News,* July 12, 2009.

Ferrell, Mary. "Ghost Stories on Campus." *Tropolitan,* October 30, 2014.

*Gainesville Independent,* March 6, 1858.

"Ghosts of Birmingham's morbidly fascinating and violent past." *Weld for Birmingham,* October 27, 2011.

Kershaw, Sarah. "Amid the Ghosts of Alabama." *New York Times,* April 18, 2008.

Naylor, Robert, Jr. "I'm Glad They're Dead. I Only Wish I'd Been There." *Meridian Star,* November 7, 1978.

Nelson, Stephanie. "Ghostbusters." *Andalusia Star-News,* July 10, 2009.

Oller, Lindy. "Opelika's Spring Villa, a place of beauty and mystery." *Opelika-Auburn News*, April 27, 2015.

"Searching for the Ghosts of Old Cahawba." *Selma Times Journal,* October 17, 2009.

Stallworth, Clarke. "River Tragedy Was Episode in Love Story." *Birmingham News*, March 9, 1975.

*Sumter County Whig,* January 4, 1853.

## Online Sources

Adventurebibleschool.com. "The Lyric Theatre of Birmingham,

Alabama." Accessed March 12, 2016. http://www.adventurebible school.com/the-lyric-theatre/.

Alabama Architecture. "Jemison-Van De Graaff Mansion." Accessed March 15, 2016. http://architecture.ua.edu/jemison-van-de-graaff-mansion/.

Alabama Ghostlore. "Brown Hall." Accessed June 5, 2016. http://facstaff.uwa.edu/abrown/brownhall.htm.

———. "Burrelson/McIntire House." Accessed June 12, 2016. http://facstaff.uwa.edu/eabrown/burrelson.htm.

———. "Cedarhurst." Accessed July 2, 2016. http://facstaff.uwa.edu/abrown/Cedarhurst.htm.

———. "Gaineswood." Accessed June 2, 2016. http://facstaff.uwa.edu/abrown/Gaineswood.htm.

———. "King House." Accessed August 3, 2016. http://facstaff.uwa.edu/abrown/kinghouse.htm.

———. "Main Residence Hall." Accessed August 3, 2016. http://facstaff.uwa.edu/abrown/mainresid.htm.

———. "Palmer Hall." Accessed August 3, 2016. http://facstaff.uwa.edu/abrown/palmerhall.htm.

———. "Reynolds Hall." Accessed August 3, 2016. http://facstaff.uwa.edu/abrown/reynolds.htm.

———. "Sloss Furnaces." Accessed June 20, 2016. http://facstaff.uwa.edu/abrown/sloss.htm.

———. "Sturdivant." Accessed June 3, 2016. http://facstaff.uwa.edu/abrown/sturdivant.htm.

———. "University of North Alabama Bookstore." Accessed June 12, 2016. http://facstaff.uwa.edu/abrown/unabookstore.htm.

Alabamahauntedhouses.com. "Jemison-Van de Graaff Mansion—Tuscaloosa AL: Real Haunt." Accessed March 15, 2016. http://wwww.alabamahauntedhouses.com/real-haunt/jemisonvan-de-graaff-mansion.html.

Alabama Historical Commission. "Gaineswood." Accessed May 5, 2016. http://www.preservdal.a.org/gaineswood.aspx.

Alabama Pioneers. "Have you ever heard the story about a ghost lady dressed in white on the old Bayview Bridge in Jefferson County?"

Accessed June 20, 2016. www.alabamapioneers.com.ghost-bay-view-bridge.

———. "Lyric Theatre in Birmingham, Alabama—a treasure that is now saved." Accessed March 12, 2016. http://alabamapioneers.com/lyric-theatre#sthash.drygbjWP.dpbs.

———. "Mysterious, haunted mansion [pics and films] in Tuscaloosa has many historical connections." Accessed March 15, 2016. http://alabamapioneers.com/tuscaloosa-jemison-van-de-graaff#sthash.yGa6Gryo.dpbs.

AL.com. "Huntsville's Weeden House has spooky stories to share during Spirit House Event." Accessed June 25, 2015. www.al.com/entertainment/index.ssf/2013/10/huntsvillesweedenhouse-hass.html.

———. "Watch the trains rumble pat the Historic Huntsville Depot, just like they have since 1860." Accessed August 3, 2016. www.al.com/news/huntsville/index...watch_the_trains_rumble_past_t.html.

Athens.edu. "Our History." Accessed May 4, 2016. http://www.athens.edu/about/our-history/foreitsnews.com.

Before It's News. "The Haunted St. James Hotel of Alabama." Accessed July 3, 2016. http:/beforeitsnews.com/paranormal/2014/06/the-haunted-st-james-hotel-of-alabama-241352.html.

Birmingham Forward. "Getting Started." Accessed April 12, 2016. http://www.slossfurnaces.com/history/.

Chattahoochee Heritage. "The Legend of Spring Villa." Accessed April 1, 2016. www.chattahoocheeheritage.org/2013/12/the-legend-of-spring-villa-2/.

Civilwaralbum.com. "Decatur Alabama Civil War Sites—Civil War Album." Accessed June 7, 2016. www.civilwaralbum.com/misc17/decatur8.htm.

———. "Tuscaloosa, Alabama: Bryce Hospital." Accessed June 30, 2015. http://www.civilwaralbum.com/misc18/bryce1.htm.

———. "Tuscaloosa, Alabama: Jemison-Van de Graaff Mansion." Accessed March 15, 2016. http://www.civilwaralbum.com/misc18/tuscaloosa_jemison1.htm.

Civil War Stories. "The Anecdote of the Officer's Party at Sweetwater." Accessed March 21, 2016. http://sweetwatermansion.blogspot. com/p/civil-war-stories.html.

Deep South Magazine. "Ghosts of Huntsville." Accessed June 25, 2015. http://deepsouthmag.com/w011/10/ghosts-of-huntsville/.

Demopolistimes.com. "Area rich in ghost stories, folk lore." Accessed April 12, 2016. http://demopolistimes.com/2008/10/30/area-rich-in-ghost-stories-folk-lore/.

———. "Quieting the Unquiet Ghost of Gaineswood." Accessed May 7, 2016. http://demopolistimes.com/2011/10/11/quieting-the-unquiet-ghost-of-gaineswood/.

Eggpen.com. "Haunted America: The Ghosts of the St. James Hotel in Selma, Alabama." Accessed July 6, 2016. http://eggpen.com/haunted-america-the-ghosts-of-the-st-james-hotel-in-selma-alabama/.

Encyclopedia of Alabama. "Athens State University." Accessed May 4, 2016. www.encyclopediaofalabama.org/article/h-2982.

———. "Gaineswood National Historic Landmark." Accessed May 7, 2016. www.encyclopediaofalabama.org/article/h-3020.

———. "Hartselle." Accessed August 1, 2016. http://en.wikipedia. org/wiki/Hartselle,Alabama.

———. "Maria Howard Weeden." Accessed June 25, 2015. www. encyclopediaofalabama.org/article/h-3060.

———. "Old Cahawba." Accessed July 5, 2016. www. encyclopediaofalabama.org/article/h-1543.

———. "University of Alabama (UA)." Accessed June 29, 2016. www.encyclopediaofalabama.org/article/h-1678.

———. "University of North Alabama (UNA)." Accessed July 1, 2016. www.encyclopediaofalabama.org/article/h-3009.

ExploreSouthernHistory.com. "Fort Morgan State Historic Park." Accessed March 25, 2016. http://www.exploresouthernhistory. com/fortmorgan.html.

FrightFind. "Hotel Highland—Pickwick Hotel." Accessed July 18, 2016. http://frightfind.com/hotel-highland-pickwick-hotel/.

Fringe Paranormal. "The Paranormal at Home: Hauntings in 50

States—Alabama's Sweetwater Mansion." http://fringeparanormal.
wordpress.com/2013/09/11/the-paranormal-at-home-hauntings-
in-50-states-alabama-sweetwater-mansion/.

Ghosteyes.com. "Haunted Schools: Athens State College." Accessed
May 4, 2016.

———. "The Lyric Theatre Ghosts in Alabama." Accessed August
8, 2016. http://ghosteyes.com.

Ghost Hunters of the South. "The Oakleigh Mansion." Accessed
July 26, 2012. www.ghots.net/investigation/oakleigh-revisit.

Ghosts and Ghouls. "Child of the Lake: Birmingham's Ghost Girl."
Accessed July 18, 2016. ghostsnghouls.com/2014/11/22/child-
of-the-lake-birmingham-ghost/.

———. "Do Dead Workers Haunt Sloss Furnaces?" Accessed April
21 2016. http://ghostsnghouls.com/2014/06/02/sloss-furnaces-
haunted/.

Ghosts of America. "Gulf Shores, Alabama Ghost Sightings."
Accessed March 17, 2016. http://www.ghostsofamerica.com/3/
Alabama-Gulf-Shores-ghost-sightings.html.

Ghost Stories and Haunted Places. "Fort Morgan." Accessed
March 12, 2016. http://ghoststoriesandhauntedplaces.blogspot.
com/2011/05/ghosts-of-fort-morgan.html.

———. "The Ghost of a Girl Named Howard." Accessed June
25, 2015. http://ghoststoriesandhauntedplaces.blogspot.
com/2012/03/ghost-of-girl-named-howard.html.

———. "The Many Ghosts of Sweetwater Mansion." Accessed
March 21, 2016. http://ghoststoriesandhauntedplaces.blogspot.
com/2010/11/many-ghosts-sweetwater-mansion.html.

———. "Sloss Furnaces." Accessed April 21, 2016. http://
ghoststoriesandhauntedplaces.blogspot.com/2010/03/sloss-
furnaces.html.

Haunted Haven. "Bryce Asylum—Tuscaloosa and Northport
Alabama." Accessed June 30, 2015. http://hauntedhaven.
blogspot.com/2014/12/bryce-asylum-tuscaloosa-and-northport.
html.

HauntedHouses.com. "St. James Hotel—HauntedHouses.com."

Accessed July 3, 2016. http://hauntedhouses.com/states/al/saint_james_hotel.htm.

———. "Sturdivant Hall." Accessed March 16, 2016. http://www.hauntedhouses.com/states/al/sturdivant_hall.htm.

Haunted Places in Birmingham, AL. "Haunting of Lyric Theatre." Accessed March 12, 2016. http://hauntin.gs.liting/lyric-theatre/.

Hauntedusa.org. "Decatur, Alabama—The Unfamiliar Guests." Accessed June 7, 2016. www.hauntedusa.org>unfamiliar.

The Hotel Highland. "History of Birmingham Alabama—The Hotel Highland Downtown UAB." Accessed July 18, 2016. www.thehotelhighland.com/history/.

Houghton Memorial Library. "The Ghosts of Huntingdon College." Accessed June 30, 2016. http://libguides.huntingdon.edu/c.php?g=86556&p=556615.

Jemisonmansion.com. "The History." Accessed March 15, 2016. http://www.jemisonmansion.com/history.html.

Lastgasps.com. "Sloss Furnace Birmingham." Accessed April 21, 2016. http://lastgasps.com/page40.html.

Mystery411. "Haunted Old Covington County Jail." Accessed April 17, 2016. http://www.mystery411.com/Landing_oldcovingtoncountyjail.html.

Our Ghostly World. "Bryce Hospital." Accessed June 30, 2015. http://ourghostlyworld.blogspot.com/2012/09/bryce-hospital.html.

Pinterest. "Union Springs, AL original façade 1880 Josephine Hotel." Accessed July 10, 2016. http://www.pinterest.com/pin/2985746502768095461.

Realhaunts.com. "The St. James Hotel." Accessed July 3, 2016. http://realhaunts.com/united-states/the-st-james-hotel/.

Ripples from Sweetwater Mansion. "Sweetwater Ruins." Accessed March 21, 2016. http://ripplesfromsweeterwatermansion.blogspot.com.

Southernbellehistory. "Covington County Jail." Accessed April 19, 2016. http://southernbellehistory.wordpress.com/2009/05/07/covington-county-jail/.

Spirit Seekers. "Historical Haunts: Fort Morgan, AL." Accessed May 2, 2016. http://thespiritseekers.wordpress.com/2010/10/13/historical-haunts-fort-morgan-al/.

Timesdaily.com. "Sweetwater Mansion site of paranormal activity hunters." Accessed March 21, 2016. http://www.timesdaily.com/archives/sweetwater-mansion-site-of-paranormal-activity-hunters/article_f2262411-b43c-5bab-968f-40c95310496d.html.

Tuscaloosa Paranormal Research Group. "Jemison VandeGraaff." Accessed April 16, 2016. http://tuscaloosaparanormal.com/jemison-vandegraaff/.

———. "Lyric Theatre." Accessed March 23, 2016. http://tuscaloosaparanormal.com/lyric-theatre/.

University of Alabama. "Is Fort Morgan Haunted?" Accessed May 2, 2016. http://www.bama.us.edu/-pgelmore/fortmorganhauntedlink.html.

University of Montevallo. "History." Accessed June 29, 2016. http://www.montevallo.edu/about-um/Um-at-a-glance/history-mission/.

WAFF.com. "Is Athens State haunted by 'die-hard' alumni?" Accessed May 4, 2016. http://www.waff.com/story/23784658/is-athens-state-haunted-by-die-hard-alumni.

Walker College Foundation. "About the Walker College Foundation." Accessed July 1, 2016. Walkercollegefdn.org/about.php.

WBHM 90.3 FM. "A Visit to the Historic Lyric Theatre Before It Reopens This Thursday." Accessed March 23, 2016. http://news.wbhm.org/feature/2016/a=visit-to-the-historic-lyric-theatre-before-it-reopens-this-thursday/.

Welcome to Haunted Rooms USA. "Sweetwater Mansion, Florence, Alabama." Accessed March 21, 2016. http://www.hauntedrooms.com/haunted-places.

WIAT.com. "Is Sloss Furnace really haunted?" Accessed April 12, 2016. http://wiat.com/2015/10/29.

Wikipedia. "Bluff Hall." Accessed April 12, 2016. http://en.wikipedia.org/wiki/Bluff_Hall.

————. "Bryce Hospital." Accessed June 30, 2015. http://en.wikipedia.org/wiki/Bryce_Hospital.

————. "Helion Lodge." Accessed June 25, 2015. http://en.wikipedia.org/wiki/Helion_Lodge.

————. "Jemison-Van de Graaff Mansion." Accessed March 15, 2016. http://en.wikipedia.org/wiki/Jemison-Van_de_Graaff_Mansion.

————. "Sweetwater Mansion." Accessed March 10, 2016. http://en.wikipedia.org/wiki/Sweetwater_Mansion.

## Blogs

Cruder, Beverly. "Selma's St. James Hotel one of the most haunted places in Alabama." Strange Alabama. July 3, 2016.

Harrington, Tony. "Some Fort Morgan Goodies." WordPress.com. October 22, 2010.

Serafin, Faith. "The Historically Haunted Josephine Hotel of Union Springs, Alabama." October 8, 2013.

## Interviews

Andrews, Mary Ruth. July 8, 2016.

Bates, Ron. March 10, 2000.

Beene, Brant. August 8, 2016.

Biglane, Teresa. November 1, 2006.

Boyd, Eloise. April 21, 1993.

Collins, Olivia. April 21, 1993.

Cook, Sandra. April 5, 1998.

Decker, Pamela. October 20, 2008.

Edmonds, Lawson. April 12, 2007.

Finlay, Louis M., Jr. February 8, 1998.

Flannigan, Barbara. August 2, 2016.

Gregg, Hunter. May 15, 2016.

Hagood, Michelle. July 10, 2016.
Johnson, Dorothy. February 7, 1998.
Jordan, Ray. October 21, 1995.
Kennedy, Betty. May 20, 2016.
Kilpatrick, Sharon. March 24, 2006 (e-mail).
Kirksey, Robert Hugh. March 12, 1998.
McBride, Amanda. August 2, 2016.
McCool, Nika. July 15, 2016.
McCoy, Frank. April 20, 1998.
McShane, Debbie. July 8, 2016.
Munoz, Charlie and Linda. August 10, 2016.
Nerewski, Stan. April 10, 2013.
Parkham, Robert. April 10, 1998.
Perrin, Joyce. July 9, 2016.
Pokorney, Jeff. July 9, 2016.
Ray, Linda. May 5, 2016.
Smith, McGregor. November 12, 1992.
Smith, Paige. May 5, 2016.
Snodgrass, Ed. August 9, 2016.
Snow, George. February 10, 2000.
Sowder, Sandra. June 12, 2016.
Tate, Pat. April 19, 1998.
Vice, Linda. August 6, 2015.
Wooldridge, Janie. April 19, 2014.

## Television Programs

"The Good, the Bad, and the Ghostly." *Deep South Paranormal.* Syfy. May 8, 2013.
"Lair of the Wickedest Man on Earth." *Scariest Places on Earth.* USA Network. April 20, 2001.
"Sloss Furnaces." *Ghost Adventures.* Travel Channel. November 14, 2008.
"Sloss Furnaces." *Ghost Asylum.* Destination America. April 12, 2015.
"Sloss Furnaces." *Ghost Hunters.* Syfy. November 17, 2010.

## Pamphlets

Jones, Tina Naremore. "Spence-Moon House." Sumter County Historical Society.

Whitfield, Jesse George. "Gaineswood and the Whitfields of Demopolis." Montgomery: Skinner, 1994.

## Miscellaneous

National Register of Historic Places Registration Form. "Cleveland, Stephen Beach House." Submitted March 3, 1999.